THE YOUNG CHEF

Recipes and Techniques for Kids Who Love to Cook

The Culinary Institute of America

Mark Ainsworth

Houghton Mifflin Harcourt

Boston ▪ New York

The Culinary Institute of America

President	Dr. Tim Ryan '77, CMC
Provost	Mark Erickson '77, CMC
Director of Publishing	Nathalie Fischer
Editorial Project Manager	Lisa Lahey '00
Recipe Testing Manager	Laura Monroe '12

For information about permission to reproduce selections from this book, write to
trade.permissions@hmhco.com or to Permissions, Houghton Mifflin Harcourt Publishing Company,
3 Park Avenue, 19th Floor, New York, New York 10016.

www.hmhco.com

Library of Congress Cataloging-in-Publication Data available upon request.

ISBN 978-0-470-92866-0 (paperback)

ISBN 978-0-544-64805-0 (ebook)

Book design by Tai Blanche

Illustrations by Joel Holland

Printed in the United States

DOC 10 9 8 7 6 5

4500653538

THE YOUNG CHEF

CONTENTS

INTRODUCTION AND ACKNOWLEDGMENTS

When I was growing up, it was a real treat to go out to a restaurant. Mom was the one who cooked breakfast, lunch, and dinner and she never got a break. We had to help chop vegetables, set up, and clean the table, but she was the boss of the kitchen. Dad was lucky that he worked, and aside from heating up a can of sardines on top of the stove (yuck), he never ventured into the kitchen until much later when I chose cooking as my profession.

When my mother returned to college to get her master's degree while I was still in elementary school, she announced that each of the four kids would be responsible for cooking dinner one night a week. After the initial shock of having to do more work wore off, I realized that I could do this. Mom helped by writing a recipe book of family favorites for us to work from. On Sunday night, we had to meet with her and review our game plan for cooking. It was important to her that we prepared a balanced meal that everyone would enjoy. My seven-year-old brother would almost always prepare "fancies," baked hot dogs slit down the center and stuffed with relish and cheese. My older sister was good at almost everything, while my younger sister and I specialized in macaroni and cheese and tuna melts.

Those early times in the kitchen paved the way for years of great eating and ultimately a profession to which I owe those lessons instilled in me by my mother. With great encouragement from my entire family, I choose to study at The Culinary Institute of America. It was an excellent choice and after working in the industry for many years, I returned to my alma mater to teach.

For years, as a father myself, I have wanted to write a kids' cookbook. All the skills we learn in school are used in the kitchen. Reading, math, nutrition, science, and craftsmanship can enthusiastically be practiced when using this book.

All the administration, staff, students, and faculty of The Culinary Institute of America have contributed to this book through their enthusiasm and love of food. The beautiful photographs have been crafted with great intensity and humor by one of the best, Phil Mansfield. Keeping it all organized has not been easy, and Lisa Lahey has persevered throughout the entire project. Thanks also go out to Maggie Wheeler and Ryan Welshhon for helping with the recipe testing, and to Nathalie Fischer for steering the ship throughout the long journey.

Lastly, a shout out to Patrice and especially the two best food critics I know, Darby and Kaleigh Ainsworth, my kids. These two girls tasted, tested, critiqued, and cooked all the recipes in this book and even had to work a few days during summer break on the photo shoot. Thanks, girls, I hope you like the book.

LEARNING THE BASICS

The basics of any skill, craft, or art—such as cooking—are always the most important to learn. Once mastered, these "basics" will allow for unending creativity and variation. As you become more comfortable with your skills, you'll enjoy cooking more and the quality of the food you cook will increase.

SAFETY FIRST

Working in the kitchen is fun, but it is not without hazards. You work with sharp objects and machines that can cause injury if you're not careful. It is important to ask for help or guidance from an adult if you are using equipment you are not familiar with or anything that could potentially cause injury. Food itself can also be a hazard in the kitchen. It is important to work clean, keep hands washed, and handle and store food the right way.

KEEPING FOOD SAFE

Foods are handled many times in their journeys from farm to table. But when foods are exposed to contaminants along the way, they can cause people to get sick. Simple steps in the kitchen can reduce contamination and keep food safe.

Microorganisms are small living things that can be seen only through a microscope.

Some are good for us:

- Yeast for bread
- Mold for blue cheese
- Bacteria for yogurt

Some can be harmful, and these are called pathogens:

- Viruses, like the flu
- Bacteria, like salmonella
- Parasites, which live in the bodies of animals
- Fungi, such as molds that spoil food

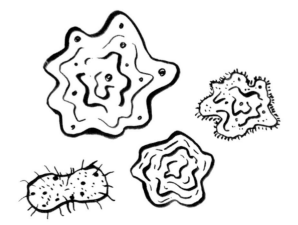

Certain types of harmful microorganisms can make us sick. When cooking, it's important to prevent harmful microorganisms from contaminating the food we eat. How we prepare and store foods can limit their exposure to pathogens in the first place, and we can also control conditions so that pathogens will not grow.

Four Ways to Keep Food Safe

1. Keep foods clean

The spread of pathogens between hands, countertops, food, cutting boards, and utensils is called **cross-contamination** and can be prevented by regularly cleaning all work surfaces, as well as by frequently washing your hands.

2. Separate raw foods from ready-to-eat

Foods that will not be cooked are considered "ready to eat" and should be kept separate from raw eggs, meat, poultry, and seafood to avoid cross-contamination. Some ready-to-eat foods include bread; raw vegetables and fresh fruits; cereal; chips, pretzels, and other snacks; and milk.

3. Cook foods thoroughly

All meats, poultry, and seafood should be cooked until they reach recommended safe minimum internal temperatures in order to kill any pathogens. Use a food thermometer to check the internal temperature (see chart, opposite page). Foods cooked in a microwave can have cold spots and should be stirred or rotated to ensure even cooking.

4. Keep foods at a safe temperature

Cooked foods are safe when they are stored in a cold refrigerator or freezer, or when they are cooked and still hot, but they are in danger of spoiling when they are kept at room temperature, between 40 and 140°F, for more than 2 hours. (This is known as the temperature danger zone.)

- Keep all cold foods stored at 40°F or below. Your refrigerator is probably set to about 35°F, which is just about right, and the freezer temperature should be at 0°F.

- Don't leave cooked foods sitting out at room temperature, or even in a warm oven, for extended periods of time while you wait to eat it.

If you're not going to eat cooked foods immediately, place them in small containers and refrigerate, then reheat when ready to eat.

Safe Minimum Internal Cooking Temperatures	
Food	**Degrees Fahrenheit (°F)**
Ground beef or pork	160
Fresh beef, veal, or lamb	145
All poultry, including chicken and turkey	165
Fresh pork and ham	145
Precooked ham (to reheat)	140
Fish	145 or until fish is opaque and flakes
Shellfish	Cook until opaque and firm

How to Use a Thermometer

Checking the temperature with a thermometer is an easy way to make sure your food is done cooking. Insert the thermometer into the center of the food, or for poultry, into the thickest part of the thigh, near the bone. Some thermometers are oven-safe, but many are not, so read the directions first. After using the thermometer, it is important to wash it to avoid possible cross-contamination the next time you use it.

KEEPING YOURSELF SAFE

Remember, the kitchen is full of things that are hot, sharp, or otherwise potentially dangerous. Always make sure an adult is nearby and get used to the following good habits to keep yourself safe:

- Wear the right clothing when cooking: Wear close-toed shoes in case a knife falls from the counter or your hand, and don't wear clothing that is very big or baggy—especially in the sleeves.

- Be careful around the stove. Always keep pot handles turned in—away from the front of the stove—so you, or someone else, can't bump into them.

- If your family has a fire extinguisher (it's a good idea to have one), learn how to use it.

- Be as careful around steam as you are around fire. Both can easily burn you.

- Keep your pets out of the kitchen while you are cooking. It is easy for them to get underfoot and cause you to trip and fall.

- Work clean. Clutter on your work surface can easily cause a knife to fall or an ingredient to spill. Wipe up spills quickly and thoroughly to make sure no one will slip.

- Take your time and concentrate. Keep your head about you. Keeping focused and undistracted allows for better judgment and is your best defense against mistakes and injury.

Washing Your Hands

Wash your hands for a full *20 seconds* using soap and hot water:

- Before and after handling food
- After using the bathroom
- After touching pets
- After being in contact with a sick person
- After blowing your nose, coughing, or sneezing
- After handling uncooked eggs or raw meat, poultry, or fish and their juices

Washing Fruits and Vegetables

- Rinse fruits and vegetables under cold running water.
- Do not use any soap or chemicals to wash fruits or vegetables.
- Even fruits and vegetables that are going to be cut need to be washed to prevent microorganisms from getting inside when you cut them.
- Scrub firm produce such as potatoes or melons with a produce brush.
- Dry all fruits and vegetables to reduce the bacteria that may still be present.

Tips to Avoid Cross-Contamination

- Place raw foods in separate plastic bags at the grocery store.
- Store raw meat, poultry, and seafood on a lower shelf than ready-to-eat foods in the refrigerator to avoid dripping juices.
- Don't use the same cutting board for raw meat and ready-to-eat foods.
- Never place cooked food back on the same plate from which it came raw.

EQUIPMENT ESSENTIALS

Take a look around your kitchen—it's most likely stocked with a treasure trove of pans, tools, and gadgets your parents have accumulated over the years. When it comes to mastering the culinary basics, however, there are only a handful of items you'll need. Take some time to scope out what you have available and use this guide to help.

POTS AND PANS

Sauté Pans and Skillets

These are used to cook tender items such as chicken, fish, eggs, and vegetables. Their sloped sides make it easy to turn the food over with a spatula or spoon.

Saucepans and Stockpots

These versatile pots can be used to boil vegetables and pastas, to cook hot cereals and grains such as rice, and to make sauces and soups.

Roasting Pans

Roasting pans are rectangular and have high sides. If you were cooking a large piece of meat, like a turkey, the juices from the food would accumulate in the bottom of the pan. These juices could then be thickened with flour or cornstarch to make a gravy or sauce. You can also use a roasting pan to roast smaller things like vegetables or small pieces of meat.

Baking Dishes

Though they are usually rectangular or oval, baking dishes can be of almost any shape and have high sides. These are used for baking foods such as macaroni and cheese or lasagna.

Baking Pans

Cookie sheets, cake pans, and muffin tins are types of baking pans used to bake things like cakes and cookies. Cookie sheets that have shallow sides are very versatile and can be used not only for cookies, but also to make thin cake layers or even to roast savory items like vegetables. Cake pans come in a variety of shapes and sizes but are most commonly round and between 7 and 9 inches in diameter.

nonstick

saucepans

Materials

Nonstick

These surfaces are very good for cooking eggs, but because the nonstick coating can become toxic when left on high heat, never leave them unattended on the stove. It is also important not to use hard metal utensils with these pans, or else you will scratch the surface. Instead, use only nylon, silicone, or wooden utensils with nonstick cookware.

Aluminum

Because it is not very heavy, aluminum doesn't conduct heat very efficiently, so your food may not cook evenly in the pan. Aluminum also reacts negatively to certain foods. For example, scrambled eggs cooked in aluminum pans will turn green, and broccoli may taste like sulfur.

Stainless Steel

Pots and pans made from stainless steel are heavy and will cook food very evenly. Additionally, stainless steel is able to withstand high temperatures and is oven-safe.

Cast Iron

These pots and pans are heavy and conduct heat efficiently. They also release small amounts of iron into the food, which is actually good for you. Before it can be used, a new cast-iron pan must be "seasoned." To do this, place the pan in a preheated 350°F oven for 20 minutes. Carefully remove it from the oven and add ¼ cup of salt to the pan. Using a pot holder and an old rag, rub the salt around and around in the pan. Discard the salt and let the pan cool down. Then coat the pan with a light film of vegetable oil. Always dry a cast-iron pan after washing, or it might rust.

Glass

Baking dishes and some saucepans are made from glass. Make sure it says "oven-ready" or "Pyrex" (a brand name), otherwise it could break at high temperatures.

KNIVES

Serrated knife

This knife has small serrations (teeth) on the edge, which allow it to cut through baked goods such as breads and cakes.

Chef's knife or French knife

An all-purpose knife used for a variety of slicing, chopping, and mincing. Chef's knives range in size from 4 to 14 inches long; a 5-inch knife is a good size for kids.

Paring knife

A short knife used for paring (trimming or peeling) fruits and vegetables.

serrated knife

8-inch chef's knife

5-inch chef's knife

paring knife

APPLIANCES

Blender

Used for making smoothies, pureeing soups and sauces, and roughly chopping nuts, vegetables, and fruits. It is dangerous to puree hot foods in the blender because the steam can get trapped and cause the lid to explode. Wait until the food has cooled slightly, or use a hand blender (see below) instead.

Food Processor

A food processor has a wider bowl than a blender and is efficient for pureeing non-liquidy foods. Many food processors also come with slicing and dicing attachments that will easily cut or shred vegetables or cheese.

Hand Blender

Also called a stick blender or immersion blender, a hand blender purees food just like a blender will, but you use it by immersing the blade end directly in the pot or bowl in which you are working. It's important to submerge the blade all the way into the food, or it will splash and cause a mess. Never turn the hand mixer on unless it is submerged in the food since it can also be dangerous and cut your hand.

Stand Mixer

This type of mixer, which features an attaching mixing bowl, typically comes with three attachments: a whip (for whipping liquid or thinner ingredients, like cream or eggs), a paddle (for mixing batters, making mashed potatoes, or working with soft but solid ingredients), and a dough hook (for heavier, thick doughs that are firm enough to knead, like yeast breads). Always make sure the bowl is secured to the base before mixing, and start the mixer on low speed.

Microwave Oven

Unlike a traditional oven, which heats food using a gas flame or electric heating element, a microwave oven produces electromagnetic waves that penetrate the food and cause water molecules to move so fast that they create friction and heat. The first microwave, sold to home cooks in the 1950s, was very large and expensive, but over time it has become small and affordable and is one of the most common kitchen appliances. It's also one of the safest because it doesn't use an open flame or exposed heating element. Best for reheating food, making popcorn, and cooking vegetables, the microwave oven is not efficient for cooking meats and fish. These foods become very tough and will not brown.

Other Useful Kitchen Equipment

Cheese grater

Colander

Cutting board(s)

Ice cream scoop

Instant-read thermometer

Ladle

Measuring cups (dry and liquid)

Measuring spoons

Metal spoons (slotted and solid)

Pot holders

Potato masher

Rolling pin

Rubber spatula

Salad spinner

Sifter

Spatulas

Strainer (fine-mesh)

Tongs

Whisk

Wooden spoons

fine-mesh
strainer

nylon spatula for use
with nonstick pans

ESSENTIAL TECHNIQUES

These techniques are the cornerstone of every chef's success. The better practiced you are at these methods, the better a chef you will become—and the better your food will look and taste.

KNIFE SKILLS

A chef's skill with a knife helps him or her work quickly and efficiently with accuracy. Precise and uniform knife cuts are one of the keys to beautiful-looking food.

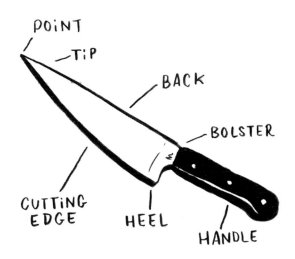

POINT

TIP

BACK

BOLSTER

CUTTING EDGE

HEEL

HANDLE

Handling a Chef's Knife

Your hand should be placed at the point where the blade and the handle meet. Hold the food with a claw-like grip. Angle your fingers down and make sure your thumb is tucked in behind your index finger.

Cut the food with even knife strokes from the tip to the heel of the knife. While cutting, rest the broad side of the knife's blade against your three middle fingers. Move the hand that is holding the food in place back little by little as you cut back along the food.

Knife Safety

Understanding how to use and maintain knives and other kitchen tools is an important part of working in the kitchen and essential to your own safety. You may need to talk to your parents before using kitchen knives. Here are some important rules:

- Keep knives sharp. A dull knife can be dangerous and make you more likely to cut yourself.
- Keep knives clean and dry. Dirty knives can cause cross-contamination.
- Store knives in a knife block, on a magnetic strip, or in a drawer with plastic knife sheaths so that they are stable and the blades are protected.
- Use the right knife for the job.

- Never put knives into a sink full of water. They can be hidden and could cut someone who reaches into the water.
- Make sure your cutting board is stable and not hanging over the edge of the counter. You can secure a cutting board on the counter by putting a wet paper towel underneath.
- Never pass a knife to someone; always lay it safely on the counter to be picked up.

Chopping an Onion

Cut the onion in half, leaving part of the root attached, and peel the onion. (The root end will look rough, with little stringy roots sticking out.)

Hold the onion half to stabilize it while you cut through the onion from top to bottom. The width of your slices will determine the final size of the pieces. Make widely spaced cuts to dice or closely spaced cuts to mince. Do not cut through the back (the root end) of the onion.

Next, cut through the onion several times from front to back.

Last, cut down crosswise through both cuts to dice or mince the onion.

Why Do Onions Make You Cry?

When an onion is cut, it releases an enzyme, known as lachrymatory factor synthase, which irritates eyes and makes us cry. You can minimize the effect by placing onions in the freezer or refrigerator for 30 minutes before you peel and cut them, or cut the onions in half and run them under cold water before slicing or chopping. You can also wear glasses or goggles to minimize the enzyme's contact with your eyes.

Peeling and Chopping Garlic

If you want slices of whole garlic cloves, cut away the root end of each clove and peel the skin from the garlic with a paring knife before slicing the clove.

If you are chopping the garlic, place the clove on the cutting board and place the flat, broad side of the knife's blade on top, and then hit it with the open palm of your hand to smash the garlic. The paper skin will fall away. Remove all of the skin and chop the garlic as finely as you want.

Glossary of Knife Cuts

Slicing

Cutting in a straight downward motion at regular intervals so that the pieces are uniform in size.

Julienne

Cutting into long, uniform "sticks" (pictured below). Accomplished by first squaring off the sides of the vegetable to make a rectangle. The "block" is cut lengthwise into slices, and then the slices are stacked neatly and cut into sticks.

Dicing

Cutting into uniform cubes. After cutting into julienne sticks, gather the sticks and cut them crosswise into small cubes.

Foods can be diced into large (¾ inch), medium (about ⅓ inch), or small (¼ inch) pieces, or very tiny (⅛ inch) pieces, which chefs call brunoise.

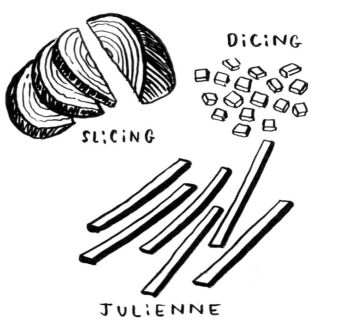

SLICING

DICING

JULIENNE

julienned vegetables

MEASURING AND MISE EN PLACE

Mise en Place

Mise en place (pronounced "meez en plas") is a French term that means "everything in its place." In the kitchen, it is a concept that helps chefs become more organized and work more efficiently. Having good mise en place means that you have cut, chopped, and measured all the ingredients needed for a recipe before you begin to cook or bake. When you have all your ingredients in front of you, the next step is to review them against the recipe to make sure nothing has been left out and that everything is measured correctly. This organizational concept will allow you to build professional-level work habits that will last forever.

Measuring

Accurate measuring is extremely important to the success of all recipes. Oftentimes just a little bit too much or too little of something can ruin the recipe.

All recipes in this book use standard US measuring spoons and cups. There are two types of measuring cups. Dry ingredients use a cup that has a flush rim and that measures exactly the amount stated on the handle. Typically these come in sets containing ⅛-cup, ¼-cup, ⅓-cup, ½-cup, and 1-cup measures. Liquid or fluid measuring cups are clear and have the measurements marked on the side of the container.

Measurement Equivalents						
3 teaspoons	=	1 tablespoon				
2 tablespoons	=	1 fluid ounce				
4 tablespoons	=	¼ cup				
8 tablespoons	=	½ cup				
16 tablespoons	=	8 ounces	=	1 cup		
2 cups	=	1 pint				
4 cups	=	2 pints	=	1 quart		
16 cups	=	4 quarts	=	1 gallon	=	128 fluid ounces
16 ounces (weight)	=	1 pound				

Measuring

When measuring dry ingredients, scoop, do not pack, the ingredient into the cup, and then level it off with the back of a knife.

When measuring liquid ingredients, place the cup on a level surface, fill it to the desired amount, and then bend down and look closely at eye level to make sure the ingredient is level with the line on the cup.

mise en place for
chicken stir fry

COOKING METHODS

The method you choose for preparing your food is just as important as the ingredients. Different cooking methods develop different flavors and textures and ultimately shape the outcome. To make successful dishes it is also important to understand that certain cooking methods are better suited to some ingredients than others. Trying out and understanding these cooking methods is a great way to learn how to cook:

- Sautéing
- Stir frying
- Pan frying
- Steaming
- Grilling
- Roasting
- Baking

SAUTÉING

To sauté you start with a hot pan and add a little fat (like olive oil or butter). Then you add the food you want to cook. It is a quick way to cook tender pieces of meat, fish, and vegetables (like chicken breast, shrimp or trout, and onions or spinach). Sautéing is similar to stir frying (see page 28); the only substantial difference is the type of pan that is used.

When sautéing, make sure you don't add too much food to the pan—this would lower the cooking temperature, and you want your pan to stay hot. Instead, when you want to sauté a lot of food, or if you only have a small pan, work in multiple batches.

One of the great things about sautéing is that a sauce can be made from the bits and pieces that get stuck to the pan. In French these bits are called **fond,** and they are the foundation of the sauce.

Equipment

The right pan for sautéing is a sauté pan, or skillet. The sloped sides of a sauté pan make it easy to turn food over with a spatula while cooking. Heavy pans are best since they conduct heat evenly, allowing for better cooking and easier cleanup. Inexpensive nonstick pans don't work well for high-heat cooking since they do not brown the food very well.

Ingredients

Many types of meats, seafood, and vegetables are good for sautéing. Use tender cuts of meat and types of vegetables, but they also have to be of the right size. If the food you are sautéing is too big or thick, it will burn on the outside before it is cooked through. All the pieces should be the same thickness and size, otherwise some pieces will cook faster than others. Meat should be cut to an individual portion size or smaller. Ideal foods for sautéing include:

- Chicken
- Turkey breast
- Beef
- Pork
- Fish fillets
- Shellfish
- Vegetables
- Tofu

Fats and Oils for Sautéing, Stir Frying, and Pan Frying

Oil gives food a nice color and texture, and has nutritional value (it's a fat; see page 44). Use only as much oil as needed to keep the food from sticking to the pan.

Types of good oils that can be used for sautéing, stir frying, and pan frying include:

- Olive oil
- Canola oil
- Peanut oil
- Nut oils
- Sunflower oil
- Safflower oil
- Pan spray

Sautéing Step by Step

Boneless, skinless chicken breasts are shown in these photos and are great for sautéing. To serve this as a meal, cook 1 breast per person, and serve the sautéed chicken with the tomato sauce on page 27.

Season each chicken breast with salt and pepper. Lightly coating the chicken with flour helps it to brown. (This is optional and not necessary for every food.) Heat the sauté pan over medium-high heat and add just enough oil to coat the bottom of the pan so the meat does not stick. When the oil just begins to smoke, place the chicken in the pan.

Cook the chicken until it is golden brown on one side and lifts easily from the pan, then flip. You want the food to be golden brown on each side.

The chicken is fully cooked when it is golden brown and a thermometer inserted into the center reaches 165°F. Letting the chicken rest for a few minutes in a warm spot while you finish cooking the rest of your meal allows the juices to cool slightly, keeping the meat much juicier. While the chicken is resting, you can make a sauce from the fond in the pan to serve with it (see page 27).

Kitchen Vocabulary

Tender foods are easy to cut and bite. Some foods are tender by nature and can easily be eaten raw — think of almost any vegetable you would put in a fresh green salad. Other tender foods require cooking (like scallops or pork chops) or just taste good when cooked (like snow peas or zucchini); these should be cooked only briefly so that they don't become too soft or mushy. Some foods are tough when raw (like some cuts of meat) but can be cooked until tender. This can take a long time — hours!

Fun Fact

Did you know that the word *sauté* is a French word that means "jump"? It is used in ballet to describe a jump off two feet, landing in the same place.

Safety First

Always wash your hands after touching raw chicken. Use a pair of tongs to place the chicken in the pan.

Kitchen Vocabulary

Fond: Small pieces of food that get stuck to the pan during cooking, which then add flavor when making a sauce.

Deglazing: Adding liquid to a pan after cooking to lift off the fond when making a sauce or gravy.

PAN SAUCES

Sauce adds flavor, moisture, texture, and even spiciness to food.

A unique aspect of sautéed and stir-fried dishes is that delicious sauces can be made from the bits and pieces (called *fond* in French) left in the pan after the food is cooked. The sauce begins when some liquid is added to the pan. This lifts the fond off the pan, a process called **deglazing.** To make a sauce using this fond, first you remove any excess fat. Then you add ingredients for flavor (aromatics), and for garnish (flavor, texture, and visual appeal). Finally you add more liquid, such as stock or broth, and thicken the sauce to the right consistency.

You want your sauce to have the right consistency, or thickness. Sauces can be thickened in a variety of ways:

- Reduced by simmering until thickened
- Pureed in a blender
- Simmered with a slurry

A **slurry** is a mixture of water and starch. Typically, water and cornstarch or flour are mixed together, then added to the simmering sauce to thicken it.

Cornstarch: To thicken 2 cups of sauce, mix 2 tablespoons cornstarch with ¼ cup water. Pour the slurry into the simmering sauce and cook for at least 1 minute.

Flour: To thicken 2 cups of sauce, mix ¼ cup flour with ⅓ cup water. Pour the slurry into the simmering sauce and cook for at least 1 minute.

Aromatic Ingredients that Can Form the Base of a Sauce

- Onions
- Peppers
- Garlic
- Fresh ginger
- Tomatoes or tomato paste
- Carrots
- Celery
- Leeks
- Beans

Liquids that Can Be Used to Deglaze the Pan

- Stock
- Fruit juice
- Water
- Milk or cream
- Tomatoes

Fun Fact

In medieval times, when there was no refrigeration and food spoiled quickly, sauces were used to mask the sour taste of spoiled meat.

Kitchen Vocabulary

Aromatics: Ingredients such as herbs, spices, or vegetables used to enhance the flavor and aroma of food.

Caramelize: The process of browning foods using high heat. When foods caramelize, their natural sugars brown, creating delicious flavors and colors. Sautéed onions and French fries are examples of foods that have been caramelized.

Reducing: Boiling a liquid, such as a sauce, to thicken it, concentrate the flavors, and decrease the volume.

Slurry: A mixture of cold water and cornstarch or flour used to thicken sauces and gravies.

Making a Fresh Tomato Sauce in the Sauté Pan

With the heat on low, add chopped onions and garlic to the pan with the fond and cook them for several minutes until they are lightly **caramelized,** or browned. Depending on the type of sauce you are making, you could also add a wide variety of ingredients—such as diced bell pepper or dried herbs like thyme or oregano—to the pan at this point. This group of ingredients is known as **aromatics** and adds a base of flavor to the sauce.

Add chopped tomatoes to the pan—depending on the season, you can use fresh or canned—and any other liquid such as water or stock. This step acts to **deglaze,** or lift off the fond from the pan, adding the flavor of the fond to the sauce.

Keep cooking the sauce until it gets thicker and **reduces** in volume. Once the sauce has reduced down to a consistency that will coat the chicken, add fresh basil or other fresh herbs, grated cheese, salt, and pepper for the final finish of flavor. Adding these ingredients at the end of cooking keeps these flavors bright and "forward" in the sauce, whereas cooking them longer would cause their flavors to be absorbed.

spoon the sauce over the chicken to serve

STIR FRYING

Stir frying is an Asian cooking technique that quickly cooks small pieces of vegetables, meats, poultry, seafood, or noodles over very high heat in a wok or sauté pan.

Equipment

Woks have a distinctive bowl-shaped form and are made by hammering large round sheets of thin steel over a circular mold. They are designed to cook bite-sized pieces of meat and vegetables quickly using little fuel and cooking oil—the thin steel allows heat to pass through the metal and into the food very quickly. Because of this rapid heat transfer, the food is constantly moved around the wok using two large spoons or wok tools to keep it from burning. In addition to stir frying, you could also steam, boil, or fry foods in a wok, making it one of the most versatile pieces of equipment in the kitchen. But if you do not have a wok, you can use a large sauté pan or cast-iron skillet to stir fry.

Ingredients

Cut ingredients for stir frying into bite-sized pieces so that they cook very quickly. Ideal ingredients for stir frying include:

- Lean chicken, turkey, beef, and pork
- Shrimp, scallops, calamari, and lobster
- Vegetables
- Noodles
- Tofu

Sauces and Seasonings for Stir Frying

The Asian kitchen is full of many wonderful premade sauces that make it easy to develop your own recipes: Just add them to your stir fry near the end of cooking. You can get most of these ingredients at the supermarket:

- Soy sauce
- Oyster sauce
- Hoisin sauce
- Shrimp paste
- Sesame oil
- Curry sauce or paste

Chef's Note

Since high heat is so important for this cooking method, never stir fry more than about a quart of food at a time to be sure the food cooks evenly and doesn't get too mushy. Work in batches if you need to cook a larger quantity.

Garlic, Ginger, and Scallions

Most Chinese-style stir-fry dishes begin with garlic, ginger, and scallions (green onions), which chefs have nicknamed "GGS." Use equal amounts of fresh ginger and garlic, and 3 times as much sliced scallions. Once the oil in the wok or pan is very hot, add the GGS and stir fry briefly before adding your other ingredients.

Have Everything Ready

Stir frying is a very quick cooking method, so it's important to have all your ingredients ready before you start. If you are not prepared, it will make for disastrous results! The food in the pan will not wait for you to prep the next ingredient and will burn or become mushy.

Stir Frying Step by Step

Chop the aromatics (garlic, ginger, and scallions) and cut up the vegetables and chicken (or other ingredients). Keep everything separate and line the bowls up on the counter so that they're easily accessible when it's time to add each ingredient to the pan.

Heat the wok over high heat, add the oil, and tilt the pan so that the oil covers the entire cooking surface of the pan. Allow a moment for the oil to get very hot, and then add the "GGS" or other aromatics. Stir them in the pan while cooking until they release their aromas.

Add the chicken and stir fry, moving it around the pan so that it cooks evenly and does not burn.

Add the vegetables and stir fry until tender. The texture of the finished vegetables will depend on what you start out with. Some vegetables, like eggplant or zucchini, will be relatively soft, while others, such as bok choy, should still be crisp to the bite.

Add aromatics and liquid ingredients to make a sauce and bring the sauce to a boil. If you want, thicken the sauce with a slurry of cornstarch and water (see page 26): Use about 1 tablespoon cornstarch mixed with 1 tablespoon water for every cup of liquid in your sauce.

PAN FRYING

Pan frying is a cooking method that cooks foods in hot oil. The food, generally small or tender pieces of meats, seafood, or vegetables, often gets coated in bread crumbs or batter before it's fried. Pan-fried foods should be crispy on the outside and moist and juicy in the middle.

Equipment

The best pan to use is a high-sided sauté pan to keep the oil from splashing or splattering as you cook.

Ingredients

The main ingredient for a pan-fried dish should be portion-sized or smaller and is often breaded before cooking for a crispy exterior. Good choices for pan frying include:

- Pork loin
- Chicken or turkey breast
- Fish
- Shellfish
- Vegetables

Mise en Place for Standard Breading Procedure

Vegetables and meats are often coated in breading before pan frying to give them a crispy outer crust. Applying breading can be a messy business, so chefs use an orderly procedure. First, coat the food lightly with flour, then dip it in beaten eggs (sometimes mixed with a bit of milk), then dip it in the breading mixture.

Breading ingredients include:

- Bread crumbs
- Crushed up crackers
- Crushed up corn flakes

Pan Frying Step by Step

Cut the chicken breasts in half and season with salt and pepper. Dip the chicken in the flour, then the egg, then the bread crumbs.

Heat the pan and the oil before adding the food. As a rule, there should be enough oil in the pan to come half to two-thirds of the way up the side of the food. Carefully place the chicken in the oil. When the bottom is golden brown, turn the chicken over and cook the other side. Continue to cook until the other side is golden brown and completely cooked; a thermometer inserted into the center should read 165°F.

Chef's Note

First, test the oil's temperature by dropping a small amount of bread crumbs into the oil. It's hot enough when the bread crumbs bubble.

Making Bread Crumbs

You can make your own bread crumbs. It's best to start with stale or day-old bread. Break or cut the bread into pieces that will fit in a food processor. Place the bread, by itself or with a bit of salt and other seasonings (such as herbs or garlic or onion powder), into the bowl of the food processor, and pulse until the bread is finely ground. Store the bread crumbs in an airtight container or bag in the freezer.

STEAMING

Steaming uses the vapor from boiling water to cook foods. Steaming cooks foods quickly, so they retain more of their natural flavors and nutrients.

Equipment

The basic way to steam foods is to put them in a metal steamer basket or insert and set it in a pot of boiling water. When the pot is covered with a lid, the steam is trapped inside and cooks the food. Bamboo steaming baskets, popular in China, are designed to fit in a wok or sauté pan. The food is placed in the covered basket and steam travels up to the food.

Ingredients

The best foods for steaming are naturally tender and small enough to be cooked in a short amount of time:

- Chicken breast
- Vegetables
- Fish fillets or whole fish
- Shellfish, lobster, clams, mussels, or shrimp

Although water is the most common liquid used for steaming, you could steam foods over other liquids, such as stock, or add aromatic ingredients, such as herbs, spices, or citrus peels or juice, to the liquid to add more flavor.

Steaming

Place the vegetables in the steamer in a single layer so that the steam will fully surround them for even cooking. Set a pan of water over the heat and bring to a simmer. Place the steamer basket or insert over the pan of simmering water. Cover the steamer to trap the steam. Cook until the vegetables are tender and bright in color.

GRILLING

Grilling is an easy, quick, nutritious, and flavorful way to cook lean pieces of meat, poultry, seafood, and vegetables. Wood, gas, or charcoal heats the grill bars and cooks the food, imparting a smoked, charred taste. Sometimes the foods are seasoned (sprinkled or rubbed with salt and pepper and/or spices) or marinated (soaked in a flavorful liquid) before grilling.

Equipment

You might have a gas or charcoal grill in your backyard. A gas grill is fueled by propane and has knobs for controlling the temperature. A charcoal grill burns charcoal; you control the temperature by using more or less charcoal and by arranging it under the grate so that some parts of the grate are closer to the charcoal than others. Whichever one you use, always have an adult light the grill.

Ingredients

When choosing items to grill, remember that grilling is a quick cooking method, so the pieces should be portion-sized or smaller. Ideal ingredients for grilling include:

- Chicken (remove the skin to keep it from burning)
- Firm-fleshed fish like salmon and swordfish
- Pork loin and pork chops
- Tender beef steaks
- Hamburgers
- Sausages and hot dogs
- Soft vegetables such as zucchini, pepper, and eggplant (but not hard vegetables such as carrots and broccoli)

Grilled foods can be marinated using:

- Spices
- Salt and pepper
- Mustard
- Small amounts of oil
- Steak sauce
- Barbeque sauce

Grilling Step by Step

Use a wire grill brush to clean the grill before you start to heat it up. Most gas grills have 2 or 3 separate temperature controls. Turn one to high, one to medium, and the last to low. Place the marinated salmon smooth side down on the section of the grill that is set to high heat. After a few minutes, to get traditional-looking grill marks, rotate the salmon about 90 degrees (called a quarter turn).

After several minutes, turn the salmon over and place it on the section of the grill set at medium temperature. This way the salmon will cook slowly, without burning, and stay juicy. To test for doneness, insert a thermometer into the center of the fish; it should read 140 to 145°F. Alternatively, press down on the top of the fish. When it is fully cooked, the fish will separate, or flake apart.

Kitchen Vocabulary

Lean meat can be from any animal; "lean" means it contains less fat than other cuts of meat. By definition, lean meat is a 3½-ounce portion that contains less than 10 grams of total fat, less than 4 grams of saturated fat, and less than 95 milligrams of cholesterol. Some of the most typical lean cuts of meat are beef sirloin, pork loin chops, and chicken breast.

Marinating food means immersing it in a liquid before cooking it in order to add flavor and moisture; the liquid is called a **marinade.** The food must be completely immersed in the marinade for at least an hour or up to overnight in order to absorb its characteristics.

Safety First

It is important to cook all ground meats until the juices run clear because hamburgers and other ground meats can be contaminated with bacteria that make people sick. See page 11 for the recommended cooking temperatures.

Remember, have an adult light the grill.

Fun Facts

- Charcoal is made from burned wood that is compressed into briquettes or cut into chunks.
- Henry Ford, founder of the Ford motor company, created the charcoal briquette from the leftover wood scraps from his automobile factories.

What Is in a Hot Dog?

Hot dogs are a pureed mixture of meat, fat, water, spices, salt, binders (usually dry milk) to hold everything together, and sometimes chemicals called nitrates. This mixture is forced into long sheep intestines, called casings, before being smoked and cooked in a water bath or steamer. Hot dogs contain about 25 percent fat and are high in salt.

- All-meat hot dogs may have beef, chicken, turkey, or pork in the mix.
- All-beef hot dogs must contain only beef.
- Kosher hot dogs are made only from beef.

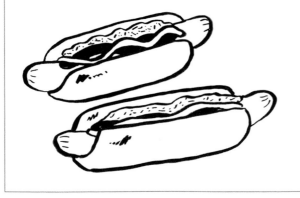

ROASTING

Roasting means cooking food in the oven. It is a great way to cook a wide variety of foods including meat, poultry, seafood, and vegetables. Both whole foods, like a whole chicken, and individual pieces, like chicken breasts or drumsticks, can be roasted. You can also make a sauce, or pan gravy, from the drippings in the pan, and serve it on the side.

Equipment

For larger items, use a heavy-bottomed roasting pan with high sides. If you're cooking a larger item, like a whole chicken, you should set it on a rack inside the pan. This lifts the roast off the pan so air can get underneath for even cooking. If you don't have a rack, you can "make" one by arranging a combination of carrots, onions, and celery (a combination known as **mirepoix**) on the bottom of the pan and setting the roast on top. The added benefit is that these vegetables then add flavor to the pan sauce. If you are cooking small pieces, such as potato wedges or other vegetables, you don't need a pan with high sides or a rack. For items such as these, a rimmed baking sheet will work just fine.

Ingredients

Foods for roasting may be left as large, whole pieces or cut smaller and combined with other ingredients. The size of the item to be roasted will determine the roasting temperature and time. For large pieces, a high temperature can cause burning on the outside before the food is fully cooked inside, while smaller items roasted at too low a temperature will cook through before they fully develop color and flavor on the outside. Good choices for roasting include:

- Chicken
- Fish
- Pork
- Beef
- Vegetables

Sauces and Pan Gravies

Just like you can make a pan sauce after sautéing (see page 26), you can also make a sauce or gravy in the pan after roasting. Sauces are typically made by adding stock to the pan drippings and can be thickened with cornstarch or flour or by cooking until reduced.

Oven temperature

Follow this very simple approach to determine what oven temperature to use.

Food Weight	Oven Temperature
0 to 2 pounds	400°F
3 to 4 pounds	375°F
4 to 10 pounds	350°F
10 to 20 pounds	325 to 350°F

Roasting Step By Step

The vegetables that you roast in the pan with the chicken can be served as a side dish.

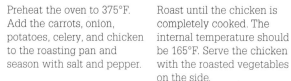

Preheat the oven to 375°F. Add the carrots, onion, potatoes, celery, and chicken to the roasting pan and season with salt and pepper.

Roast until the chicken is completely cooked. The internal temperature should be 165°F. Serve the chicken with the roasted vegetables on the side.

Making Gravy

If you want to make a gravy to serve with your roast chicken, put the roasting pan on the stovetop and stir in the flour. Cook on low heat for several minutes. Whisk in the stock. Simmer until the gravy is smooth and thick, 5 to 10 minutes.

Carryover Cooking

Food will continue to cook a bit more even after it's removed from the heat. This is especially true for roasted foods.

BAKING

Baking is a craft that has been practiced for thousands of years to make breads, cakes, and pastries.

Equipment

For baking you will need any number of specific baking pans, such as loaf pans, cake pans, cookie sheets, or cupcake pans. For most recipes, you will want a stand mixer or handheld electric mixer to do some of the "heavy lifting" of mixing ingredients, which will give you better results and also cut down considerably on preparation time. Other tools for baking include wooden spoons, rubber spatulas, rolling pins, and measuring cups and spoons.

Ingredients

The basic ingredients used in baking can be combined and mixed in many different ways to produce finished foods that have very little in common, from a cream puff to a loaf of challah bread. Each ingredient plays a different role in determining the characteristics of the finished food. Ingredients used for baking include:

- Flour
- Fats (butter or oil)
- Eggs
- Sugar
- Liquids
- Leaveners

Flour

Flour gives strength and structure to baked goods. Flour has protein in it, and when flour is mixed with water, protein strands (called gluten) form. The gluten is like a scaffolding or web that gives the baked goods their shape.

Eggs

Eggs provide structure and stability to baked goods because as they bake in the batter or dough, they become solid and bind the other ingredients together. When whipped, eggs trap air bubbles that expand when heated, making the finished product light and airy.

Types of Flour

Different types of flour have varying amounts of protein and starch. The protein forms gluten when moisture is added. A flour with high protein creates a dough that is tough and elastic, which is good for things like yeasted breads. A flour that has less protein and more starch is better for things like cake, which we want to be soft and tender. You can buy bread flour, which is high in protein, or cake or pastry flours, which are low in protein, but all-purpose flour is the best choice for the recipes in this book. It has a medium protein content and is the best all-around flour.

Gluten and Fat

Gluten is a protein that is present in flour. As a dough or batter is mixed, the gluten in the flour is developed, but different baked goods require different amounts of gluten to have the texture and flavor that we want: a good baguette is crisp on the outside and chewy on the inside (lots of gluten), a chocolate chip cookie is chewy and moist with crispy edges (moderate amount of gluten), and a layer cake is moist and tender, not chewy at all (practically no gluten). When you add fat to a dough or batter, it coats the developing strands of gluten and makes them shorter, which makes the finished food more tender.

Sugar

Sugar attracts and bonds with water, and for this reason it makes and keeps baked goods moist. Since it attracts all the water, it also keeps baked goods tender by keeping the water away from the developing gluten — gluten (see opposite page) needs water to form.

Sugar also helps beaten fats, eggs, and egg whites trap air bubbles, which makes baked goods light and fluffy. It browns during cooking or baking, which adds color and flavor. And you know that gooey top that you love on your banana bread and muffins, and that crispy top on your pound cake and brownies? Well, that is sugar too. As the water evaporates from the tops of these treats during baking, the sugar is left behind to do its thing — be melty and gooey, or recrystallize and become crunchy.

Liquids

Water, milk, and other liquids work to dilute or liquefy and distribute ingredients such as sugar and salt throughout a batter or dough. Liquid acts as a leavener (see below) when it changes to steam and expands.

Fats

Fats tenderize baked goods by coating the strands of gluten, which can otherwise make doughs and batters tough, as they develop, making them shorter and not as tough. Butter is the most common fat used in baking, but some recipes use oil or shortening.

Leaveners

To **leaven** is to rise, or to make lighter. In baking, leavening is what makes breads or cakes fluffy, with holes of air inside. There are several ways to leaven in baking: with yeast, with chemicals such as baking powder or baking soda, or with steam from liquid in the recipe.

Egg Whites

When whipped, egg whites become light and fluffy and puff up in volume. This is because they contain a protein that, when whipped, creates small balloon-like structures that hold air and stick together to create volume. When whipping egg whites, be sure that your bowl is very clean because if there is any fat or egg yolk in the bowl, the whites will not whip.

Other Sweeteners

- Corn syrup is processed from corn starch into a thick, heavy syrup that does not crystallize.

- Honey is made by bees, who work diligently gathering nectar from flowers, traveling millions of combined miles to produce just 1 gallon of honey. Twice as sweet as sugar, honey has many unique qualities. It is not affected by bacteria, and when stored in a dry environment it can last for thousands of years. But because honey is a liquid, it is not easy to substitute for sugar in a recipe. It is **hygroscopic** (meaning it attracts moisture), so it causes food to brown more than regular sugar. Doctors recommend that children less than one year old should not eat honey.

- Molasses is thick dark syrup made by boiling the liquid residue from crushed sugar cane. It has a rich, caramelized, slightly bitter and acidic flavor and is an excellent ingredient for baking cookies.

HOW TO COOK FLAVORFUL FOOD

Making delicious food involves choosing ingredients that taste great together. This can be accomplished by combining foods' flavors and textures in different ways.

How We Taste

Taste Buds

When you look at the surface of your tongue in the mirror, you will see that it is covered in little bumps that are called papillae fungiform. These delicate bumps contain taste buds and temperature receptors that interact with the compounds found in food. These cells immediately send the taste information to our brain, where we interpret the information and make decisions about how we think the food tastes. The average person has over 10,000 taste buds. Because kids have more taste buds on their tongues than adults, they are better tasters. Luckily, taste buds regenerate every couple of weeks, but after age forty this regeneration slowly decreases. The five primary tastes that our taste buds detect are sweet, sour, salty, bitter, and umami.

But flavor is a complex sensation produced by more than just taste—it's a combination of taste and aroma.

Taste + Aroma = Flavor

The nose contains olfactory receptors, which are cells that send aroma information to the brain. When we chew food, chemicals are released and rise up from our mouths into our nostrils, triggering the olfactory receptors. Our brains then process the information from the taste buds and olfactory receptors to create the true flavor of the food.

When you lose your sense of smell, it limits flavor and therefore also limits your desire to enjoy food. If you've had allergies or a cold, then you might have noticed this loss of flavor when your nose was stuffy.

Creating Flavors in Food

When you cook, you create depth and dimension by varying the proportions of the five primary flavors as you decide what ingredients to use. Each individual taste interacts with other tastes by either complementing or contrasting their basic characteristics.

Here are some common ingredients that reflect each of the five primary tastes:

Sweet Ingredients

- Fruits
- Ketchup
- Sugar
- Honey
- Chocolate
- Syrups
- Jams and jellies
- Barbeque sauce

Sour Ingredients

- Citrus
- Vinegar
- Yogurt
- Sauerkraut
- Pickles
- Sour cream

Salty Ingredients

- Salt
- Cured meats like bacon and salami
- Soy sauce
- Cheese
- Snack foods like chips, nuts, and pretzels
- Olives

Bitter Ingredients

- Arugula
- Coffee
- Kale
- Grapefruit

- Bitter chocolate
- Horseradish
- Watercress

Umami-Rich Ingredients

- Steak
- Fermented foods like miso paste
- Soy sauce
- Mushrooms
- Tomatoes

- Aged cheeses like Parmesan
- Cured foods like cured ham
- Celery
- Green tea
- Seaweed

Complementing flavors are similar flavors that blend well. Think of making a fruit salad. All of the individual fruit flavors are delicious on their own, but they are all bright, fresh, sweet, and a little acidic, so they also blend together well. Or think of mushroom gravy with roast beef and mashed potatoes. All of these flavors are warm, rich, and earthy. They all complement each other because of their similarities.

When opposite—**contrasting**—flavors and textures are combined and eaten together, they support each other and create a unique and appealing eating experience. There are many examples of this in the foods we eat every day:

- Peanut butter + jelly = rich and creamy with sweet and sour
- Hot dog + relish, mustard, or sauerkraut = salty and fatty with sweet and sour
- Crème brûlée = rich and creamy with sweet, crispy, and caramelized
- Kettle corn = crispy, salty, and sweet
- Fried fish + tartar sauce = crispy and fatty with sour

Building Flavor Through the Use of Aromatic Ingredients

Aromatics are flavorful ingredients used to begin the cooking of many of our favorite dishes. They are called aromatics because they bolster the flavor and aroma of a dish. Onions, garlic, celery, carrots, ginger, peppers, tomatoes, and spices are often cooked as the first step of a recipe in order to "build" flavor. Onions and garlic are two of the most commonly combined foods in the kitchen. They can serve as the main flavoring (for example, onion soup), but more often they are used as

Building a Vocabulary to Describe Flavor and Texture

These words are commonly used to describe foods' tastes and textures. Learning these words will help you communicate the language of food. What are some other words you might use to describe food?

Sweet: Sugary, Syrupy

Sour: Tangy, Tart, Acidic

Bitter: Harsh, Acrid

Salty: Over-salted

Fatty: Oily, Buttery, Greasy, Slippery

Starchy: Floury, Gluey, Granular

Pungent: Overpowering, Heady, Strong, Spicy

Spicy: Hot, Piquant, Peppery, Fiery, Zesty

Fruity: Tropical, Fresh, Floral, Citric

Chemical: Metallic, Ammonia, Soapy

Rancid: Putrid, Foul, Off, Sour, Spoiled

Coarse: Grainy, Rough

Thick: Gooey, Gelatinous

Smooth: Soft, Creamy

Creamy: Smooth, Buttery, Silky, Soft

Crispy: Crackly, Hard, Crunchy

Hard: Firm, Ridged

foundational aromatic and flavoring ingredients. They add depth of savory flavor as well as sweetness.

There are two ways to cook aromatics:

Sweating means to cook them over low heat so that the moisture in the food is slowly released without the food turning brown.

Browning occurs at higher heat, when the sugars in the food heat up and caramelize (see page 26). This will develop the flavor as well as the texture of the aromatics, releasing sweet flavors from the sugars and sometimes creating a crispy outer edge. When browning garlic in particular, it is best to heat it slowly over low heat so it does not become bitter.

Roasted Garlic

Roasting garlic develops its rich, sweet flavors, leaving the spicy flavor behind. It also renders each clove of garlic as spreadable as soft butter (in fact, you can use it in the same way you'd use butter — squeeze a roasted clove to remove the papery skin, spread it on a slice of Italian bread or baguette, and sprinkle with a hint of salt). Preheat the oven to 350°F. Cut a bulb of garlic in half crosswise and pour ½ teaspoon of oil on the open face of each clove. Wrap the garlic in aluminum foil and bake for 30 to 45 minutes or until the garlic is soft. Let the garlic cool and then squeeze it out of the skin.

Seasoning

The process of **seasoning** involves adding an ingredient to give foods a particular flavor. Common seasonings include salt, pepper, herbs, spices, and condiments. To season "to taste" means to taste the food as you add the seasonings and stop when the food tastes best to you.

International Flavors

Each cuisine has ingredients and flavors that make it distinct. If you like a particular cuisine, you can introduce its flavor into almost anything you make by adding combinations of common seasonings from that region or country. Some examples of common regional flavors include:

Mexico: Cumin, chili powder, garlic, cilantro, coriander, oregano, lime

Asia: Ginger, garlic, scallions, soy sauce, sesame seeds and oil, star anise, fish sauce, oyster sauce

Greece: Lemon, allspice, garlic, olive oil, rosemary, thyme, oregano

Caribbean: Lime, allspice, garlic, peppers, thyme, scallions, curry

Italy: Tomatoes, olives and olive oil, garlic, basil, oregano, fennel, red wine vinegar

Spain: Saffron, garlic, olive oil, parsley, cumin, ham, chorizo sausage

HOW FOOD FUELS YOUR BODY

Your body is like a machine that needs fuel to continuously generate energy. Foods that are important for energy contain different amounts of carbohydrates, proteins, and fats. Eating a wide variety of different-colored foods (called the "rainbow diet") is an easy way to get the right balance of these core nutrients.

The Food Groups

The main food groups are fruits, vegetables, grains (like bread, rice, or cereal), proteins (like meat, tofu, or eggs), and dairy (like milk, cheese, or yogurt). A balanced diet means eating the right amounts, and the right mix, of food groups.

Recommended Servings for Kids

Fruits: 1 to 2 cups per day

Vegetables: 2 to 3 cups per day

Grains: 3 slices of whole-grain bread or 1½ to 3 cups grains per day

Protein: 5 to 6.5 ounces per day

Dairy: 1½ to 3 cups milk per day

Sugars and fats occur naturally in these foods, but extra sugars and fats (like those found in desserts or snack foods) should be limited.

It is also best to limit highly-processed foods. Processing really can mean doing anything to foods — chopping and cooking can be considered processing — but packaged foods and fast foods are usually highly processed. Generally speaking, the more a food has been processed, the more unhealthy ingredients, like sugar or preservatives, may have been added, and the more naturally-occurring nutrients may have been removed.

Calories

A calorie is a unit of measure just like an inch or a pound, but rather than measure length or weight, a calorie measures energy. Knowing how many calories are in food helps us understand how much energy our bodies will gain from eating it. If we use up fewer calories than we eat, our bodies store the extra energy as fat for later use. If we eat fewer calories than we need, our bodies will then access the excess calories we have stored as fat and use them. Kids between the ages of ten and fourteen generally need to consume about 1,600 to 2,600 calories per day. If you play sports or are very active, you might need to eat even more.

7 Building Blocks of Smart Eating

- Eat fresh foods that are minimally processed.
- Eat mostly plant-based foods: fruits, vegetables, whole grains, beans, and nuts.
- Eat smaller amounts of meat, poultry, and dairy products.
- Reduce consumption of animal fats; choose mostly plant oils.
- Control and understand proper portion sizes.
- Use salt with care and purpose; don't over-salt.
- Be physically active.

What Are Nutrients?

The three "macro" nutrients are carbohydrates, protein, and fat. Carbohydrates are used by your body to produce the fuel it needs to give you energy. This fuel can be used immediately or stored by your body for future use. Protein (from a Greek word, *proteios*, that means "of prime importance") is responsible for your body's growth, fluid balance, and energy. Fat is used by your body to store energy, insulate organs and bones, and promote the absorption and storage of certain vitamins.

Foods that are high in carbohydrates include fruits, bread and grains, starchy vegetables (like potatoes and carrots), and beans. Foods that are high in protein include meat, poultry, seafood, eggs, tofu, beans, and dairy. Foods that are high in fat include meat, butter and oils, cheese, and some dairy.

Fiber

Fiber is found in fruits and vegetables. It is the portion that our bodies can't break down and digest or absorb as nutrients and use, so it passes through our systems virtually intact. But fiber serves a very important role in the health of our bodies. As it passes through, it takes with it all kinds of other waste that otherwise would move very slowly through our system. Foods rich in fiber include raspberries, pears (with skin), bananas, oranges, barley, oatmeal, popcorn, black beans, almonds, artichokes, broccoli, and potatoes.

Antioxidants and Phytochemicals

Antioxidants and **phytochemicals** are compounds that occur naturally in grains, vegetables, fruits, and legumes. It is thought that plants produce these compounds to help combat diseases such as viruses, fungi, and bacteria. When we consume these plants, we benefit from these nutrients in the same way they do. They help to fight cell damage and may also reduce the risk of cancer, heart disease, and chronic ailments. Individual plants have different types and amounts of these chemicals, which are often represented by the color of the plants. Generally speaking, colorful fruits and vegetables contain the highest amounts of antioxidants, so consuming a rainbow of colors throughout the day is a smart way to eat.

What Are Whole Grains?

A **whole grain** (sometimes referred to as the kernel) is the entire seed of a plant and is made up of three parts: the germ, the endosperm, and the bran. The germ is actually the embryo, which, if fertilized by pollen, could sprout into a new plant. It is one of the healthiest parts of the grain, containing high amounts of vitamins, proteins, and good fats. The endosperm is the largest part of the grain; it is the germ's food supply and contains large amounts of starchy carbohydrates and minimal amounts of vitamins. The bran is the kernel's protective layer and contains healthy vitamins and fiber. When grains are refined into flours, the germ and bran are often removed, leaving only the least nutritious part of the grain. Whole grains are less refined, so they contain large amounts of vitamins, minerals, and nutrients.

Fat: The Good and the Bad

Fat is an important nutrient for good health. It's important for heart health, learning and memory, cushioning our internal organs and keeping us warm, and helping in nerve function, nutrient absorption, and building cell membranes. However, some fats are better for you than others, and too much fat is not good for you. "Good fats" are liquid at room temperature and come from plants (like nuts, seeds, avocados, and olives) and from fish. "Bad fats" are solid at room temperature and come from red meats, butter, whole milk and cream, and cheeses.

- Try to get your fats from lean meats, fish, nuts and seeds, and vegetable and nut oils.
- Eat less meat, especially beef and pork.
- Limit fried foods, packaged foods, and desserts.
- Choose low-fat dairy products.

Vitamins and Minerals

Vitamins and minerals are important to our bodies' functions, including disease prevention and maintenance. Some important vitamins and minerals include:

Vitamin or Mineral	Functions	Found in
Vitamin A	Helps with bone and tooth growth and vision, fights infection, and may prevent certain cancers	Animal products and orange, yellow, and dark leafy green vegetables The body can make it using beta-carotene
Vitamin B-complex	Helps with energy production, skin health, and digestion	Animal products only
Vitamin C	Helps with fighting infection, healing cuts and wounds, absorbing iron from foods, and building blood vessels, may protect against heart disease and cancer	Strawberries, citrus fruits, kiwis, peppers, Brussels sprouts, broccoli, tomatoes
Vitamin D	Helps with bone and tooth growth, promotes overall growth	Sunlight Cereals, milk, and some other foods are fortified with vitamin D
Vitamin E	Protects cell membranes, may help fight cancer	Wheat germ, almonds, sunflower seeds, peanut butter, spinach, broccoli
Vitamin K	Regulates calcium levels, regulates blood clotting	Leafy green vegetables, Brussels sprouts, broccoli, fish, plums, yogurt
Calcium	Promotes bone growth and healthy muscles and heart tissues	Dairy, beans, oats, almonds, cabbage, broccoli, oranges
Iron	Helps move oxygen to the cells	Bran flakes, oatmeal, lentils, chickpeas, soybeans, figs, pumpkin and pumpkin seeds, red meat, eggs, turkey, shellfish, Swiss chard, sweet potatoes
Magnesium	Helps the body use protein	Oats, wheat, artichokes, milk, yogurt, beans, almonds, spinach
Phosphorus	Maintains healthy bones and muscle function	Bran, beef, nuts, chicken, dried fruits, eggs, garlic, beans, fish, yogurt
Zinc	Assists in metabolism and protects the immune system	Beef, pumpkin seeds, sesame seeds, wheat germ, peanuts, cocoa powder, oysters

RECIPES

Now that you understand the essential cooking techniques, these recipes—besides making delicious meals for you to eat—are opportunities to practice what you've learned. They're also opportunities to think creatively: You should always feel free to experiment with your favorite ingredients and come up with new ideas. That's a big part of what being a chef is about!

BREAKFAST

chocolate and banana
breakfast shake

ON-THE-GO CEREAL BALLS

Makes 6 balls (6 servings)

- 3 cups of your favorite cereal
- ¾ cup peanut butter or other nut butter
- ¾ cup nonfat powdered milk (see Chef's Note)
- ½ cup honey
- ¼ cup chopped dried fruit (optional)
- ¼ teaspoon vanilla extract

1. Lightly crush the cereal in a medium bowl, and then add the peanut butter, powdered milk, honey, dried fruit, if using, and vanilla. Mix until the cereal is evenly coated.

2. Use your hands to shape the mixture into 6 balls. Eat right away, or refrigerate, covered, until ready to eat.

Chef's Note
Powdered milk is made by dehydrating (removing the water from) liquid milk. This form of milk has many uses, but in a recipe like this, it helps hold all of the pieces together. You can find powdered milk at your grocery store.

HIGH-PROTEIN CHOCOLATE AND BANANA BREAKFAST SHAKES

Makes about 2 cups (2 servings)

- 1 cup ice
- 2 tablespoons sugar
- 1 tablespoon cocoa powder
- ½ cup silken tofu
- 1 banana
- ¼ cup low-fat yogurt
- ¼ cup low-fat milk or soy milk

1. In a blender, combine the ice, sugar, cocoa powder, tofu, banana, yogurt, and milk. Blend on high speed until the shake is combined and creamy.

2. Serve the smoothies right away in chilled tall glasses.

Chef's Note
You could also add wheat germ, flax seeds, dried fruit, or nuts (soaked in water first, to soften them) for additional flavor, texture, and nutritional value.

Healthy Start
Tofu is packed with protein, which helps to make this filling smoothie a great start to your day. It also helps to make the smoothie extra creamy!

Safety First
Remember to never put your hands inside the blender when it is plugged in. If you need to stir the ingredients, stop the blender, take the pitcher off of its stand, and use a long spoon.

PEACH SMOOTHIES

Makes about 2 cups (2 servings)

2 medium ripe peaches, peeled and pit removed (see Chef's Notes)
1 medium banana, sliced (see Chef's Notes)
1 cup peach juice or nectar
½ cup plain yogurt
2 tablespoons honey (optional)

1. In a blender, combine the peaches, banana, peach juice or nectar, yogurt, and honey, if using. Blend until smooth and thick.

2. Serve the smoothies right away in chilled tall glasses.

Chef's Notes

If you can't find sweet, fresh peaches, substitute 1 cup of frozen peach slices — no need to defrost!

You can also keep peeled bananas in the freezer for ease of use. Using frozen bananas will change any smoothie into a frosty treat.

What Are Flaxseeds and Chia Seeds?

Flaxseeds (also called linseeds) are a rich source of nutrients (vitamins and minerals like manganese and vitamin B1), fiber, and a healthy fatty acid known as Omega-3. The seeds come from flax — the same fiber used to make linen fabric and one of the oldest fiber crops in the world, known to have been cultivated in ancient Egypt and China. Chia is a tasteless seed from a plant found in Mexico and Guatemala. Besides adding great texture, both flax and chia seeds offer an opportunity to get more nutrients without changing the the taste of your smoothie.

Think Like a Chef

Smoothies are an easy way to experiment with different flavors since you can make a smoothie out of almost any ingredient. Choose fruits and vegetables that complement each other, like sweet berries with tart lime juice, plus a little liquid to help them blend smoothly. And remember that fruity flavors can overpower the flavor of some vegetables, so don't be afraid to put some spinach in your blender!

Blueberry and Peach Smoothie: peaches + blueberries + yogurt + juice + flax seed

Green Smoothie: spinach + green apple + kiwi + honey

Tropical Fruit Smoothie: papaya + mango + banana + coconut water

How to Cut a Mango

A mango has a pit in the center, so when cutting into the fruit, you have to estimate where you think the pit is. As you slice, you will be able to feel if your knife is hitting the pit, so just adjust as you go. Carefully slice down the sides of the mango (the parts that look like cheeks), as close to the pit as possible, to remove the two ears of flesh from the mango. Score the flesh in a cross-hatch pattern, without cutting through the skin. Turn the ear of flesh inside out, then cut away the cubes from the skin.

STRAWBERRY SMOOTHIES

Makes about 5 cups (3 servings)

2 cups ice

1 cup orange or pineapple juice

8 medium-sized fresh strawberries

2 tablespoons honey (optional)

1. In a blender, combine the ice, juice, strawberries, and honey, if using. Blend until smooth and thick.

2. Serve the smoothies right away in chilled tall glasses.

Chef's Note

If you can't find sweet, fresh strawberries, substitute frozen strawberries—no need to defrost!

GRANOLA

Makes 5 cups (about 6 servings)

1½ cups rolled oats

¼ cup canola oil

¼ cup light brown sugar

¼ cup honey

2 teaspoons ground cinnamon

½ cup sunflower seeds

½ cup sweetened shredded coconut

¼ cup wheat germ

¼ cup sesame seeds

¼ cup chopped almonds

¼ cup chopped walnuts

½ cup raisins

1. Preheat the oven to 300°F.

2. Combine the oats, oil, sugar, honey, and cinnamon. Spread the mixture into an even layer on a cookie sheet and bake for about 20 minutes, until fragrant and lightly toasted, stirring occasionally.

3. Add the sunflower seeds, coconut, wheat germ, sesame seeds, almonds, and walnuts to the mixture in the pan. Toss together and spread into an even layer on the pan, and then bake for about 15 minutes more, or until all of the ingredients are golden brown. Remove the pan from the oven, add the raisins, and let the granola cool completely.

4. Store in an airtight container. Serve with milk or yogurt and fresh fruit.

Think like a Chef

Chocolate, dried fruits, and seeds are great additions to granola, and it's easy to mix and match! After the granola cools, mix in your favorites, like chocolate chips, pumpkin seeds, dried mango, or dried cranberries.

* * * * *

You've eaten granola for breakfast — but how else can you use it?

- Sprinkled over ice cream

- As part of a snack mix, with dried fruits, pretzels, and chocolate chips

- Crumbled on top of a baked apple with cinnamon and whipped cream

- Mixed into a smoothie for some crunch

EGGS IN A BASKET

Makes 4 servings

4 bread slices

2 tablespoons butter

4 eggs

Salt, to taste

1. Butter one side of each slice of bread and stamp a hole in the middle of each slice with a cup or cookie cutter that is about 3 inches in diameter.

2. Place the slices of bread in a cool nonstick pan, butter side down (you may have to work in batches if you can't fit all four slices of bread in your pan at one time). Place the pan over medium heat. While the pan is heating, crack one of the eggs and put it into a small bowl or ramekin.

3. Once the pan is hot, slowly drop the egg from the bowl or ramekin into the hole in one of the bread slices. If it goes in slowly, it will set as it is poured in and will not leak out from under the slice of bread. Season the egg with a pinch of salt. Repeat with the remaining eggs and cook over medium heat until the eggs have set, 2 to 3 minutes.

4. Once the eggs are firm enough, carefully flip the bread and the eggs over using a spatula, and cook for several minutes on the other side, until the eggs are cooked to your desired doneness, about 30 seconds for runny yolks and about 1 minute for firm yolks. Serve immediately.

Chef's Note

You could also scramble the eggs in a bowl first instead of adding them whole. Pour them into the holes in the bread in Step 3 and continue with the rest of the recipe. If you are scrambling the eggs, you could also mix in cheese, tomatoes, peppers, ham, or almost any of your other favorite omelet ingredients. Just remember to cut the ingredients into small bites so that they cook quickly.

How Would You Like Your Egg?

Hard boiled: cooked in boiling water in the shell until the entire egg, white and yolk, is completely solid, or "hard."

Soft boiled: cooked in boiling water in the shell until the egg white is hard and the yolk is left runny, or "soft."

Poached: cooked in boiling water out of the shell until the egg white is firm and the yolk is still warm and runny.

Sunny-side up: cooked in a greased frying pan until the underside is done and the yolk is warm and runny. The egg is never flipped for a sunny-side-up egg.

Over easy: cooked in a greased frying pan until the underside is done and then flipped to cook the egg white on both sides, leaving the yolk warm and runny.

Over medium: cooked in a greased frying pan until the underside is done and then flipped to cook the egg white on both sides, leaving the yolk only slightly runny.

Over hard: cooked in a greased frying pan until the underside is done and then flipped to cook the egg white on both sides and the yolk in the center until both are cooked through.

Scrambled: cracked into a bowl and whisked until the white and yolk are completely blended together, then cooked in a greased frying pan while stirring occasionally until firm.

FRENCH TOAST

Makes 6 slices (3 servings)

3 eggs

¼ cup milk

1 teaspoon vanilla extract

1 teaspoon sugar

½ teaspoon salt

1 tablespoon butter or vegetable oil

6 slices bread (see Chef's Note)

1. In a mixing bowl, combine the eggs, milk, vanilla, sugar, and salt.

2. Heat the butter or oil on a nonstick griddle or in a large frying pan over medium heat.

3. Dip each slice of bread in the egg mixture, gently pressing and flipping so that both sides are fully coated and the bread has absorbed some of the egg mixture.

4. Place the egg-soaked bread onto the griddle or into the hot pan. You may need to work in batches if you can't fit all of the bread into your pan at once.

5. Cook the French toast until it is golden brown on one side, about 2 minutes, and then flip it using a spatula and cook until the other side is golden brown, about 2 minutes more. Serve with syrup, powdered sugar, or fresh fruit.

Chef's Note

You can use any bread to make French Toast, but slices of a rich, buttery bread like brioche, challah, or cinnamon-raisin bread can make your breakfast extra special. Since the bread is a little bit denser than typical sandwich bread, allow the slices to sit in the egg mixture for a few seconds, to help it soak up more moisture.

WAFFLES

Makes 4 to 6 waffles (depending on the size of your waffle iron)

1¾ cups all-purpose flour

¼ cup wheat germ (see Chef's Note)

1 tablespoon baking powder

1 tablespoon sugar

¼ teaspoon salt

1¾ cups milk

2 eggs

3 tablespoons vegetable oil, plus more as needed for greasing the waffle iron

1. In a medium bowl, mix together the flour, wheat germ, baking powder, sugar, and salt.

2. In a separate bowl, whisk together the milk, eggs, and oil.

3. Pour the milk mixture into the flour mixture and mix until the ingredients are just combined, but do not over mix (some small clumps of flour are fine).

4. Heat the waffle iron and carefully brush it with oil.

5. Ladle the batter into the waffle iron and close the lid. The amount of batter and the time it takes to cook will depend on the type of waffle iron you are using. The finished waffle should be crisp and golden brown. Serve with syrup or fresh fruit.

Chef's Note

Like the flour you typically use, wheat germ comes from wheat kernels but from a different part—the germ, which is the center of the kernel. Unlike all-purpose flour, which is refined into a very fine powder, wheat germ is coarse. It is added to this recipe for extra texture, flavor, and nutrition, but you could use all-purpose or whole-wheat flour instead.

CHEESY SCRAMBLED EGGS

Makes 4 servings

8 eggs

¼ cup milk

¼ teaspoon salt

Pinch of ground black pepper

1 tablespoon butter or vegetable oil

½ cup grated cheese, like cheddar

1. In a mixing bowl, combine the eggs, milk, salt, and pepper. Beat with a whisk until combined.

2. Meanwhile, heat the butter or oil in a large nonstick sauté pan over medium heat.

3. Add the egg mixture to the hot pan and cook, stirring with a heat-safe rubber spatula, until large firm pieces form, about 5 minutes. The eggs should be firm, but not dry.

4. Add the cheese to the eggs in the pan and mix until it is fully incorporated and melted. Remove from the heat and serve immediately.

Chef's Note

When choosing your cheese, make sure you use a semi-soft cheese that is good for melting, such as cheddar, Monterey Jack, or Swiss.

Fun Fact

How many eggs does a chicken lay in a day? The typical range is one or two a day, but sometimes NONE! The factors that affect how many eggs a chicken will lay are:

- The time of year (chickens will stop laying eggs entirely in the winter unless you leave a light on and trick them into feeling like the days are longer)

- The breed of the chicken (some are excellent layers and some are not)

- The age of the chicken (chickens start laying eggs when they are about 6 months old and stop when they are around 5 years old)

- When chickens are molting, they lay fewer eggs

- Happy chickens lay more eggs!

Think Like a Chef

You can add other ingredients to scrambled eggs too. Meats and some vegetables should be already cooked. Onions and peppers, for example, should be sautéed first to develop flavor and soften them a bit; spinach should be sautéed to soften it and remove some of its moisture. All ingredients should be relatively dry, as you don't want to add extra liquid—this would make your eggs runny.

Greek Scrambled Eggs:
feta cheese + spinach + roasted peppers

Chilaquiles-Style Scramble:
sliced onions + black beans + green tomatillo salsa + tortilla chips + cheddar cheese

Denver-Style Eggs:
ham + bell pepper + onion + cheddar cheese

Mushroom Scrambled Eggs:
mushrooms + spinach + Swiss cheese

OPEN-FACED OMELET WITH TOMATO AND MOZZARELLA

Makes 1 omelet (2 to 4 servings)

4 eggs

1 tablespoon milk

¾ teaspoon salt

Pinch of ground black pepper

½ cup chopped tomatoes

½ cup shredded mozzarella cheese

1 tablespoon unsalted butter or vegetable oil

1. In a mixing bowl, combine the eggs, milk, salt, and pepper. Beat with a whisk until combined and then stir in the tomatoes and cheese.

2. Heat the butter or oil in a small nonstick sauté pan over medium heat.

3. Add the egg mixture to the hot pan and use a heat-resistant rubber spatula or wooden spoon to gently stir and evenly spread the ingredients. Cook until the eggs are nearly set, about 30 seconds.

4. Use a pancake spatula to flip the eggs over and cook until the eggs are fully cooked, about 1 minute.

5. Transfer the finished omelet to a plate and cut into wedges to serve.

Chef's Note
You could also add other ingredients, such as ham, bacon, and peppers or other vegetables, to the omelet.

Cooking Bacon
Want some bacon with your eggs? To cook it, place the bacon in a pan over low heat. The bacon will begin to release some of its fat as it is heated and will then cook in its own fat. The bacon will bubble, buckle, and curl as it cooks. Cook until it is brown on one side, then turn it over with a fork or tongs and cook until the other side is brown. If you are cooking a lot of bacon, cook it in batches, making sure not to overcrowd the pan, and pour off excess fat.

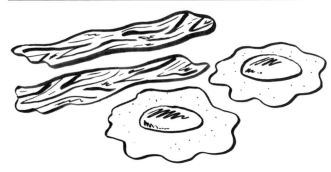

PANCAKES

Makes about 12 pancakes (about 4 servings)

2 cups all-purpose flour
2 tablespoons sugar
2½ teaspoons baking powder
½ teaspoon salt
2 eggs
1¾ cups milk
1 tablespoon melted butter, plus more as needed for greasing the pan

1. In a mixing bowl, whisk together the flour, sugar, baking powder, and salt.

2. In a separate bowl, whisk together the eggs, milk, and melted butter.

3. Pour the egg mixture into the flour mixture and mix until the ingredients are just combined, but do not over mix (some small clumps of flour are fine).

4. Preheat a griddle or frying pan over medium heat and grease with butter.

5. Ladle about ¼ cup of batter for each pancake onto the griddle or hot pan, being careful to leave enough room for the batter to spread and for you to flip the pancakes. You will need to work in batches to make sure you don't overcrowd the griddle or pan, and you want to make sure you have a little room to make flipping easier. When bubbles begin to break on the surface of the pancakes, after about 1 minute, flip each pancake and cook until golden brown on the other side, 1 to 2 minutes more. Serve with syrup, powdered sugar, or fresh fruit.

Add-Ins

Fold ½ cup mini chocolate chips or 1 cup blueberries into the finished batter before cooking.

Think Like a Chef

What else could you add to pancakes to change their flavors?

Spiced Pumpkin Pancakes: pumpkin puree + cinnamon + nutmeg + candied ginger

Sweet and Savory Pancakes: cooked bacon + scallions + cheddar cheese

Sunflower Pancakes: whole wheat flour (instead of all-purpose flour) + wheat bran + sunflower seeds + honey

Variation
CARAMEL APPLE PANCAKES

Cook some diced apples in a saucepan with a little butter until soft. Drizzle your pancakes with store-bought caramel sauce and top them with the apples, a few walnuts, a sprinkling of sea salt, and some whipped cream (see page 180).

BLUEBERRY MUFFINS

Makes 12 muffins

2 cups plus 2 tablespoons all-purpose flour

1½ teaspoons baking powder

½ teaspoon salt

¼ teaspoon nutmeg

¾ cup milk

1 large egg

½ teaspoon vanilla extract

½ cup (1 stick) unsalted butter, at room temperature, plus more as needed for greasing the pan

1 cup sugar

1½ cups fresh blueberries, washed and patted dry, or unthawed frozen blueberries

1. Preheat the oven to 400°F.

2. Prepare one 12-cup muffin pan or two 6-cup muffin pans by greasing them or by using muffin papers.

3. Whisk together 2 cups of the flour and the baking powder, salt, and nutmeg in a bowl. In a separate bowl, whisk together the milk, egg, and vanilla.

4. Using a mixer, beat together the butter and sugar until light and smooth in texture, 3 to 4 minutes. Add the flour mixture in 3 additions, alternating with the wet ingredients, mixing on low speed. Scrape down the side of the bowl with a rubber spatula a few times to make sure everything blends evenly. Raise the speed to medium and mix until just incorporated, about 1 minute.

5. In a separate bowl, sprinkle the remaining 2 tablespoons flour over the blueberries and toss to coat them evenly. Using a wooden spoon or rubber spatula, gently mix the blueberries into the batter.

6. Divide the batter among the muffin cups. Bake until the tops of the muffins are golden brown and a toothpick inserted into the center of one comes out clean, 18 to 20 minutes.

7. Let the muffins cool in the pan on a wire rack for 5 minutes. Remove them from the pan to finish cooling.

Kitchen Science

Baking soda and baking powder are the main chemical **leaveners** we use in the kitchen. When water is mixed with these products, a chemical reaction takes place, producing carbon dioxide gas. The small gas bubbles get trapped in the dough, and when exposed to heat, the gas expands. This makes the food light and airy and produces volume and texture.

The Toothpick Test

To test if a baked item is done, inserting and then removing a toothpick will help you check the condition of the interior. The recipe will let you know if it should come out "clean" or in some cases "have a few moist crumbs attached," depending on the recipe.

Think Like a Chef

When you substitute ingredients in a recipe, you want to add roughly the same amount. In this recipe, use the amount of blueberries as a guide for substituting a different "add-in." If you want to add a spice, start with a small amount, say ½ to 1 teaspoon. If you are adding sweet ingredients like honey, you will want to cut back on the sugar so that your muffins aren't too sweet. Remember to make notes of all the changes you make to a recipe so that you can reproduce the results, or "tweak" them next time you bake!

Hawaiian Muffins: pineapple chunks + shredded coconut + macadamia nuts

Chocolate-Cherry Muffins: dark chocolate chunks + dried cherries + walnuts

Honey Muffins: diced pear + ground cardamom + honey

Key West Muffins: shredded coconut + lime zest

CORN MUFFINS

Makes 12 muffins

1¼ cups all-purpose flour

½ cup cornmeal

½ cup sugar

3½ teaspoons baking powder

1 teaspoon salt

2 eggs

⅔ cup water

⅓ cup vegetable oil, plus more as needed for greasing the pan

¼ teaspoon vanilla extract

1. Preheat the oven to 350°F.

2. Prepare one 12-cup muffin pan or two 6-cup muffin pans by greasing them or by using muffin papers.

3. Whisk together the flour, cornmeal, sugar, baking powder, and salt in a bowl.

4. In a separate bowl, mix together the eggs, water, oil, and vanilla.

5. Using a whisk or an electric mixer on medium speed, mix the wet ingredients into the dry ingredients until just incorporated, about 1 minute, scraping down the bowl once. Divide the batter among the muffin cups.

6. Bake until the centers of the muffins feel springy and the tops are beginning to brown, about 20 minutes.

7. Let the muffins cool in the pan on a wire rack for about 5 minutes. Remove them from the pan to finish cooling.

Chef's Note

Have you ever thought about adding savory mix-ins to your muffins? Cheddar cheese, chopped jalapeños, and even cooked bacon are delicious in sweet corn muffins, and can be added to the batter before baking.

Kitchen Vocabulary

Greasing a pan keeps food from sticking to it. When a recipe says to grease a pan, that means to add a thin layer of butter or oil to the surface of the pan. To grease a pan, you can either lightly spray it with cooking spray or use a brush or paper towel to wipe the pan with butter or oil.

corn muffin

SOUPS, SALADS, AND SANDWICHES

Corn Chowder

Loaded Baked Potato Soup

Cream of Broccoli Soup

Egg Drop Soup

Vegetable Soup

Leftover Spaghetti and Chicken Soup

Vegetarian Chili

Coleslaw

Cold Sesame Noodles

Caesar Salad

Caesar-Style Salad Dressing

Mexican Street Corn Salad

Ranch Dressing

Tomato-Parmesan Salad Dressing

Greek Salad

Watermelon and Cucumber Salad

Grilled Cheese Sandwiches

California Club Sandwiches

Crispy Chickpea Pitas

Thanksgiving Sandwiches

Open-Faced Mushroom Tortas

Roasted Vegetable Bowls

Farro Caprese Salad

CORN CHOWDER

Makes about 8 cups (about 8 servings)

2 tablespoons vegetable oil

3 strips bacon, chopped (optional)

1½ cups chopped onion

1 cup chopped celery

¼ cup all-purpose flour

1 quart chicken or vegetable stock

3 cups fresh or frozen corn kernels
(see Chef's Note)

1 cup diced russet potato

1 tablespoon lemon juice

1½ teaspoons salt

1 teaspoon chopped fresh thyme

¼ teaspoon ground black pepper

1. Heat the oil in a soup pot over medium heat. Add the bacon, if using, and cook, stirring with a wooden spoon, until it is light brown and crispy, about 5 minutes. Add the onion and celery and cook, stirring, until the vegetables soften, about 5 minutes.

2. Add the flour and cook, stirring occasionally, until the flour becomes very thick and light brown, about 5 minutes.

3. Using a whisk, stir in the stock and cook until the soup thickens, about 10 minutes.

4. Add the corn, potatoes, lemon juice, salt, thyme, and pepper.

5. Simmer the soup until the potatoes are tender, about 30 minutes. Serve immediately.

Chef's Note

If using fresh corn from the cob, reserve the cobs after removing the corn kernels. Place the cobs in the broth as it simmers to help give the soup more corn flavor. Remove the cobs from the soup before serving.

Did You Know?

Corn is one of the world's most important grains. Its history began when early Mesoamericans began cultivating the wild plant. Early civilizations were fueled by corn and as populations increased, people had to settle near their corn fields. As people stayed close to tend to the fields, permanent villages sprang up and socialization began.

Did You Know?

Unusual products that contain corn:

- Toothpaste
- Gasoline
- Salad dressing
- Yogurt
- Chewing gum
- Shampoo
- Milk
- Soda
- Diapers
- Glue

LOADED BAKED POTATO SOUP

Makes about 4 cups (6 servings)

1 tablespoon olive oil

10 slices bacon, cut into 1-inch pieces

1¼ cups diced onion

1 cup diced yellow or white potato

1¼ cups sliced leek (white part only)

4 cups chicken broth

1 cup sour cream

2 tablespoons unsalted butter

1 teaspoon salt

½ teaspoon ground black pepper

1 cup shredded cheddar cheese

2 tablespoons chopped chives

1. Heat the oil in a soup pot over medium heat. Add the bacon and cook until it is crispy, about 6 minutes. Use a slotted spoon to remove the bacon from the pot, reserving the oil in the pot, and transfer the bacon to a paper-towel-lined plate to drain.

2. In the same pot over medium heat, add the onion and potato and cook, stirring with a wooden spoon, until the onion is golden brown, 5 to 7 minutes. Add the leek and cook until the leek begins to soften, about 3 minutes.

3. Add the broth and bring to a simmer over medium-low heat. Cook until the potatoes are tender, about 25 minutes.

4. Use a stick blender, or let the soup cool slightly and then use a food processor and work in batches, to puree the soup. You can blend it as much as you like, depending on whether you like a very smooth soup or one that is a little bit chunky.

5. Remove from the heat and stir in the sour cream and butter. Season with the salt and pepper.

6. Spoon the hot soup into bowls and garnish with the cheese, chives, and cooked bacon. Serve immediately.

Everybody Loves Bacon, but What Is It?

Bacon comes from the belly of the pig and naturally has a lot of fat. (That is why it shrinks so much during cooking—the fat melts off and is left behind in the pan.) It is cured in a mixture of salt, sugar, and spices (and sometimes a chemical called nitrate), which kills possible bacteria. After curing, bacon is smoked (placed in a closed container filled with smoke, in order to add a smoky flavor), then sliced and packaged. Look for bacon that is nitrate free for a healthier choice.

CREAM OF BROCCOLI SOUP

Makes about 6 cups (8 servings)

2 tablespoons extra-virgin olive oil
2 pounds broccoli, roughly chopped
½ cup chopped yellow onion
½ cup chopped leek
¼ cup all-purpose flour
6 cups chicken or vegetable broth
½ cup heavy cream
1 teaspoon salt
½ teaspoon ground black pepper

1. Heat the oil in a soup pot over medium heat. Add the broccoli, onion, and leek. Cook, stirring frequently, until the vegetables begin to soften, 6 to 8 minutes.

2. Add the flour and cook, stirring frequently with a wooden spoon, until the mixture thickens and the flour begins to brown slightly, about 5 minutes.

3. Add the broth to the pot slowly, whisking well to work out any lumps. Bring the soup to a simmer over medium heat, stirring frequently to prevent the bottom of the pot from burning. Cook until the soup has thickened, about 45 minutes.

4. Use a stick blender, or let the soup cool until it is barely warm and then use a food processor and work in batches to puree the soup. You can blend it as much as you like, depending on whether you like a very smooth soup or one that is a little bit chunky.

5. Add the cream, salt, and pepper, and stir to combine. Serve the soup very hot.

Variation
BROCCOLI-CHEDDAR SOUP

Stir in 2 cups of shredded cheddar cheese in Step 5.

Safety First

Using a stick blender right in the pot is the safest way to puree warm liquids. Transferring hot foods to a food processor risks burning yourself by accidently spilling the hot liquid. If you don't have a stick blender, let the liquid cool before you puree it.

EGG DROP SOUP

Makes 4 cups (4 to 6 servings)

4 cups chicken stock or vegetable stock

4 tablespoons cornstarch

¼ cup water

2 eggs, beaten

3 tablespoons chopped scallions

1 tablespoon soy sauce

1 to 2 teaspoons salt

¼ teaspoon sesame oil

1. In a soup pot over medium heat, bring the chicken stock to a simmer.

2. In a small bowl, combine the cornstarch and water and mix until there are no lumps. Slowly stir the cornstarch mixture into the simmering stock, and cook until the soup begins to thicken slightly, about 5 minutes.

3. Remove the soup from the heat and, stirring the soup while it is still hot, slowly pour in the eggs in a thin stream. The eggs will form cooked ribbons as you stir them into the soup.

4. Add the scallions, soy sauce, salt, and sesame oil. Serve immediately.

Kitchen Vocabulary

A **slurry** is a mixture of liquid (like water, broth, or juice) and a powdered starch (like cornstarch, potato starch, or tapioca starch), that is used as a thickener for soups and sauces. When starch is added directly to a hot food, like soup, it can become clumpy. So instead, it's better to add the starch to a small amount of liquid and mix it until it is smooth before pouring it into the other ingredients.

VEGETABLE SOUP

Makes about 10 cups (8 servings)

- 3 tablespoons olive oil
- 1¼ cups chopped onions
- ¾ cup chopped leek (white and light green parts)
- ⅔ cup chopped carrots
- ½ cup chopped celery
- ½ cup chopped cabbage
- 2 quarts vegetable broth
- ½ cup chopped tomatoes
- ½ cup peeled, chopped potatoes
- ½ cup fresh or frozen peas
- ½ cup fresh or frozen corn kernels
- ¼ cup chopped parsley
- ½ teaspoon dried thyme
- 1 teaspoon salt
- ¼ teaspoon ground black pepper

1. Heat the oil in a soup pot over medium heat. Add the onions, leek, carrots, celery, and cabbage. Cook, stirring frequently, until the vegetables are softened, about 15 minutes.

2. Add the broth, bring to a simmer, and cook for 10 minutes.

3. Add the tomatoes, potatoes, peas, corn, parsley, and thyme. Continue to cook until the potatoes are tender and cooked through, 10 to 15 minutes more.

4. Add the salt and pepper. Remove from the heat and serve hot.

Chef's Note

Almost any vegetable can be used in this soup, including broccoli, parsnips, sweet potatoes, and green beans. Add harder vegetables that take longer to cook (like parsnips) in Step 1, and add smaller and more delicate vegetables (like broccoli) later, in Step 3.

LEFTOVER SPAGHETTI AND CHICKEN SOUP

Makes about 2 quarts (16 servings)

2 teaspoons vegetable oil

1 cup chopped cabbage

½ cup chopped onion

½ cup chopped tomato

¼ cup chopped celery

¼ cup chopped carrot

1 teaspoon garlic powder

3 cups chicken stock

1 cup leftover cooked spaghetti

1 cup cooked, cubed chicken breast

½ cup chopped green beans

½ cup corn kernels, fresh or frozen

1 teaspoon salt

½ teaspoon dried oregano

¼ teaspoon ground black pepper

1. Heat the oil in a large soup pot over medium heat. Add the cabbage, onion, tomato, celery, carrot, and garlic powder. Cook, stirring with a wooden spoon, until the vegetables soften and begin to brown around the edges, about 15 minutes.

2. Add the stock and simmer for an additional 15 minutes to develop flavor.

3. Add the pasta, chicken, green beans, corn, salt, oregano, and pepper. Cook until all of the ingredients are very hot, 15 minutes more. Serve immediately.

Think like a Chef

Making changes to a soup is fun and easy. Use the same basic vegetables and then change the protein (such as meat, seafood, or beans) and spices, and add some different veggies. You can make adjustments to the soup as it cooks based on what you see and taste. If the soup looks too brothy, add more vegetables, meat, fish, or beans. If after you taste it, you want it more flavorful or spicy, add more herbs and spices (but it's best to add them in small increments).

Minestrone Soup: cannellini beans + leftover tomato sauce + dry or fresh oregano and thyme

Coconut Curry Noodle Soup: coconut milk + curry paste (green, red, or massaman) + shrimp + baby corn + green onion + bamboo shoots

Turkey Meatball Soup: turkey meatballs (page 108) + red bell pepper + baby spinach

Chef's Note

Many other vegetables, both fresh and frozen, can be added to this soup, such as chopped kale leaves, broccoli, bell pepper, or asparagus—or try your favorite.

VEGETARIAN CHILI

Makes about 12 cups (12 servings)

- 2 tablespoons olive oil
- ¾ cup chopped onion
- ¾ cup chopped green bell pepper
- ¾ cup chopped red bell pepper
- 3 cloves garlic, minced
- 5 tablespoons chili powder
- 1 teaspoon ground cumin
- 2 tablespoons tomato paste
- One 28-ounce can chopped tomatoes, with their juices
- One 15-ounce can black beans, drained and rinsed
- One 15-ounce can pinto beans, drained and rinsed
- One 15-ounce can chickpeas, drained and rinsed
- 2 teaspoons salt

1. Heat the oil in a large saucepan over medium heat. Add the onion and green and red bell peppers, and cook, stirring with a wooden spoon, until the onions are soft and just beginning to turn brown around the edges, about 10 minutes. Add the garlic and continue to cook, stirring, over medium heat until the garlic is fragrant, about 6 minutes more. Remove the pepper mixture from the pan and reserve in a bowl.

2. Add the chili powder and cumin to the same saucepan and stir to combine. Add the tomato paste and cook over medium heat, stirring occasionally, until it becomes slightly darker in color, about 2 minutes.

3. Add the tomatoes, black beans, pinto beans, chickpeas, and the reserved pepper mixture. Simmer gently until the vegetables are tender, about 15 minutes. If the chili looks like it is getting dry, add water ¼ cup at a time until it reaches the right consistency.

4. Add the salt and remove from the heat. Serve immediately.

Chef's Note

Chili is often served with shredded cheese and sour cream, but you can add any garnishes you would like, such as chopped scallions, cilantro, and roasted corn.

COLESLAW

Makes 4 to 6 servings

½ cup mayonnaise

¼ cup cider vinegar

2 tablespoons vegetable oil

4 teaspoons sugar

1 teaspoon salt

⅛ teaspoon ground celery seeds

⅛ teaspoon ground black pepper

7 cups (1 small head) shredded green cabbage

1. In a large bowl, mix together the mayonnaise, vinegar, oil, sugar, salt, celery seeds, and pepper.

2. Add the cabbage and mix well to incorporate all of the ingredients.

3. Serve immediately, or cover and refrigerate until ready to serve.

What Is Sriracha?

Sriracha is a 2,000-year-old hot chili sauce from Asia that is very popular in the United States today.

Think like a Chef

The term "coleslaw" does indicate a salad made of shredded cabbage. But over time, in the culinary world, the term "slaw" has evolved to mean almost any type of shredded vegetable salad. So, to "think like a chef" and make a "slaw," make sure your veggies are grated (carrots or peeled broccoli stems) or cut into fine slices to create a shred (kale or cabbage).

Carrot Slaw: carrots + honey + mustard

Mango Slaw: mangoes + red cabbage + cilantro + lime juice

Spicy Broccoli Slaw: shredded broccoli + shredded cauliflower + carrots + Sriracha

COLD SESAME NOODLES

Makes 4 servings

2½ teaspoons salt

½ pound (8 ounces) spaghetti

¼ cup creamy peanut butter

1 tablespoon sesame oil

1 tablespoon sugar

1 teaspoon cider vinegar or rice vinegar

⅛ teaspoon ground black pepper

2 tablespoons chopped scallions

1. Bring a large pot of water to a boil over high heat and add 2 teaspoons of the salt. Add the spaghetti and cook until it is tender, about 8 minutes. Drain the noodles in a colander and rinse under cold water until cooled.

2. In a microwave-safe bowl, combine the peanut butter, sesame oil, sugar, vinegar, the remaining ½ teaspoon salt, and the pepper. Microwave for about 30 seconds, until the peanut butter is melted. Stir until the ingredients are combined and smooth.

3. In a bowl, combine the cooled spaghetti and the peanut butter sauce. Top the salad with the scallions and serve cold.

CAESAR SALAD

Makes 6 servings

2 heads romaine lettuce

1½ cups croutons

½ cup grated Parmesan cheese

1 cup Caesar-Style Salad Dressing (at right)

½ teaspoon ground black pepper

1. Separate the romaine lettuce leaves. Wash the leaves and use a towel to pat them dry. Tear or cut the leaves into 1-inch pieces and place the lettuce in a large bowl.

2. Add the croutons and cheese to the bowl, and toss the ingredients until they are evenly mixed.

3. Add the dressing and pepper and toss until the lettuce is coated with the dressing and the ingredients are evenly mixed. Serve immediately.

Making Croutons

You can use store-bought croutons or you can easily make your own. Simply tear or cut a loaf of French bread into 1-inch cubes and toss with ¼ cup of olive oil, ½ teaspoon of salt, and ½ teaspoon of garlic powder. Spread the bread onto an aluminum foil–lined baking sheet and bake in a preheated 350°F oven until the croutons are golden brown and crispy.

Did You Know?

It is said that restaurateur and Italian immigrant Caesar Cardini first prepared this famous dressing tableside at one of his restaurants in Tijuana, Mexico in 1924. The original version, which he tossed over tender romaine leaves, consisted of olive oil, coddled eggs (eggs that are very briefly poached), lemon juice, Parmesan cheese, and Worcestershire sauce. Famous author and TV chef Julia Child wrote about eating Caesar's salad at his restaurant in Mexico when she was a child, which helped to increase its popularity throughout the world.

CAESAR-STYLE SALAD DRESSING

Makes 2 cups

1½ cups mayonnaise

¼ cup sour cream

¼ cup grated Parmesan cheese

¼ cup water

3 tablespoons lemon juice

½ teaspoon garlic powder

½ teaspoon sugar

¼ teaspoon onion powder

¼ teaspoon salt

Pinch of ground black pepper

1. In a mixing bowl, combine the mayonnaise, sour cream, cheese, water, lemon juice, garlic powder, sugar, onion powder, salt, and pepper. Whisk until well combined.

2. Transfer to a covered container and refrigerate until ready to use.

Chef's Note

This recipe makes more than you need for the Caesar Salad at left. Refrigerate any leftover dressing in a covered container to use for another salad or as a sandwich spread.

MEXICAN STREET CORN SALAD

Makes 4 to 6 servings

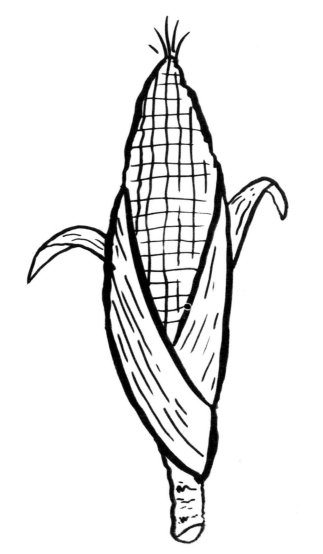

1 tablespoon vegetable oil

2 cups cooked fresh or frozen corn kernels

3 tablespoons mayonnaise

1 tablespoon lime juice

1 teaspoon ground cumin

1 cup canned black beans, drained and rinsed

¼ cup chopped cilantro

¼ teaspoon salt

¼ teaspoon ground black pepper

½ cup crumbled queso fresco cheese

1. Heat the oil in a large sauté pan over medium heat. Add the corn and cook, stirring frequently, until the corn begins to brown slightly but is still moist, about 5 minutes. Remove from the heat and let cool completely.

2. In a medium bowl, combine the mayonnaise, lime juice, and cumin. Add the cooled corn, black beans, and cilantro and mix to combine. Add the salt, pepper, and cheese and stir until all of the ingredients are evenly coated with the mayonnaise. Serve immediately.

RANCH DRESSING

Makes 3 cups

- 2 cups mayonnaise
- ½ cup buttermilk
- ½ cup sour cream
- 1 tablespoon chopped fresh parsley
- 2 teaspoons sugar
- 1½ teaspoons salt
- 1 teaspoon onion powder
- 1 teaspoon garlic powder
- ¼ teaspoon ground black pepper

1. In a medium bowl, combine the mayonnaise, buttermilk, sour cream, parsley, sugar, salt, onion powder, garlic powder, and pepper. Mix until the dressing is smooth and creamy.

2. Transfer to a covered container and refrigerate until ready to use.

Preparing Salad Greens

Any leafy tender green, such as lettuce (but also small, tender leaves of spinach or kale), can be used to make a salad. If you are starting with a whole head of lettuce: Remove the core from the lettuce using a knife. Cut or tear the lettuce into consistent-sized pieces and place them in a bowl of very cold water. The cold water will keep the leaves crispy and remove any dirt or sand. Gently wash the lettuce, being careful not to bruise the delicate leaves. Dry the lettuce in a colander or salad spinner; this will keep the leaves fresh and crisp.

TOMATO-PARMESAN SALAD DRESSING

Makes 1¼ cups

- ½ cup chopped tomato
- ¼ cup extra-virgin olive oil
- ¼ cup grated Parmesan cheese
- 2 tablespoons water
- 2 teaspoons chopped garlic
- 1 teaspoon mustard (any type)
- ½ teaspoon sugar
- ¼ teaspoon salt
- ⅛ teaspoon ground black pepper

1. In a blender, combine the tomato, oil, cheese, water, garlic, mustard, sugar, salt, and pepper. Puree until the dressing is very smooth.

2. Transfer to a covered container and refrigerate until ready to use.

GREEK SALAD

Makes 8 servings

2 tablespoons lemon juice

2 teaspoons balsamic vinegar

1 tablespoon chopped parsley

½ teaspoon salt

¼ teaspoon ground black pepper

¼ cup extra-virgin olive oil

2 heads romaine lettuce, rinsed, dried, and torn into pieces

1 cup Greek olives, cut in half lengthwise

2 cups sliced, peeled seedless cucumber

2 cups halved cherry tomatoes

1 yellow bell pepper, seeds removed, thinly sliced

1 red onion, sliced ⅛ inch thick

2¼ cups crumbled feta cheese

1. In a medium bowl, combine the lemon juice, vinegar, parsley, salt, and pepper and stir until the salt is dissolved. Slowly pour in the oil, whisking constantly, until the oil is blended into the dressing.

2. Place the romaine in a salad bowl. Add the olives, cucumber, tomatoes, bell pepper, onion, and feta. Add the dressing, and toss together until the ingredients are evenly coated. Serve immediately.

WATERMELON AND CUCUMBER SALAD

Makes 4 servings

¼ cup rice wine vinegar or white wine vinegar

2 tablespoons sugar

3 tablespoons chopped fresh mint leaves

¼ teaspoon crushed red pepper flakes (optional)

2 cups cubed watermelon (about 1-inch cubes)

1 cup thinly sliced seedless cucumbers, peel on

½ cup thinly sliced red onion

1 head Boston lettuce

1. In a small bowl, combine the vinegar, sugar, 1 tablespoon of the mint, and the red pepper flakes, if using, and refrigerate while you prepare the remaining ingredients.

2. In a large bowl, combine the watermelon, cucumbers, and onion.

3. Wash the lettuce and remove the leaves. Tear the leaves into 1-inch pieces.

4. Add the vinegar mixture to the melon and cucumbers and stir to combine. Add the lettuce and remaining 2 tablespoons of mint and toss until all of the ingredients are well combined. Serve immediately, while still very cold.

GRILLED CHEESE SANDWICHES

Makes 4 sandwiches

| 4 tablespoons (½ stick) butter |
| 8 slices bread, any kind |
| 8 slices cheese, any kind |

1. Put the butter in a microwave-safe dish and microwave it in 10-second intervals until it is fully melted.

2. Brush the butter onto one side of each slice of bread. Sandwich the bread with 2 slices of cheese for each sandwich, with the buttered sides of the bread facing out.

3. Heat a large griddle or sauté pan over medium heat. Add the sandwiches (you may need to cook the sandwiches in batches if your pan isn't large enough).

4. Cook until golden brown on one side, about 2 minutes, then flip each sandwich and cook until the other side is browned, about 2 minutes more. Serve immediately.

Think like a Chef

Grilled cheese sandwiches can be customized however you like. With the number of cheeses and the variety of breads alone—not to mention added vegetables (or fruits!)—the variations are endless. Only make sure you are not using a hard cheese that won't melt easily, like Parmesan or aged provolone. Added vegetables should be soft, like tomatoes, or precooked, like sautéed onions or spinach (a sliced crispy pickle would be fine).

Grilled Cheese with Apples: whole-grain bread + sharp cheddar cheese + Granny Smith apple slices

Sweet and Savory Grilled Cheese: sourdough bread + brie cheese + Hazelnut Chocolate Spread (page 164)

Italian-Style Grilled Cheese: mozzarella cheese + roasted red peppers + Pesto Sauce (page 143)

Pimiento Grilled Cheese: cheddar cheese + mustard + pimiento peppers

CALIFORNIA CLUB SANDWICHES

Makes 4 sandwiches

12 slices whole-grain bread, toasted

½ cup mayonnaise

1 pound sliced turkey

8 pieces cooked bacon

1 avocado, thinly sliced

1 tomato, thinly sliced

1 cup sunflower or alfalfa sprouts

1. Spread the slices of toasted bread with the mayonnaise. Top 4 of the slices with the turkey and bacon. Top the turkey and bacon with a second slice of toasted bread and then add the avocado slices, tomato slices, sprouts, and a third piece of toasted bread, mayonnaise side down.

2. Use large sandwich picks to hold the sandwiches together if you'd like, and cut each sandwich in half or into quarters. Serve the sandwiches immediately.

CRISPY CHICKPEA PITAS

Makes 6 to 8 sandwiches

Chickpea Patties

½ cup chopped onion

2 tablespoons minced garlic

One 15-ounce can chickpeas, drained

¼ cup chopped parsley

¼ cup chopped cilantro

1½ teaspoons salt

¼ teaspoon ground black pepper

¼ teaspoon ground allspice

¼ teaspoon ground coriander

2 tablespoons all-purpose flour

1 cup Hummus (page 153)

3 or 4 pita pockets, cut in half

2 tomatoes, thinly sliced

1 cucumber, thinly sliced

8 leaves Romaine lettuce

1. Preheat the oven to 400°F and lightly grease two 12-cup muffin pans.

2. To make the chickpea patties, place the onion and garlic in the bowl of a food processor, and pulse to combine, about 15 seconds. Add the chickpeas, parsley, and cilantro, and pulse again until the ingredients are well combined and finely chopped, but not pureed. Scrape the side of the bowl as needed.

3. Transfer the chickpea mixture to a large bowl and add the salt, pepper, allspice, coriander, and flour. Mix until combined.

4. Measure 2 tablespoons of chickpea batter and roll into a ball. Place the ball into a muffin pan cup and press down to create a flat patty. Repeat with the remaining chickpea batter to form a patty in each cup.

5. Bake until the patties are golden brown and semi-firm when you press them gently, about 25 minutes. Remove from the oven and gently slide the cooked patties out of the muffin pan.

6. To assemble the sandwiches, spread about 2 tablespoons of hummus inside each pita half. Fill the pockets with the tomato, cucumber, and lettuce, and then place 3 to 4 hot chickpea patties in each pocket. Serve immediately.

THANKSGIVING SANDWICHES

Makes 4 sandwiches

½ cup mayonnaise

1 tablespoon chopped sage

8 slices whole-grain bread

1 pound sliced turkey

¾ cup Cranberry Sauce (recipe follows)

1. In a small bowl, combine the mayonnaise and sage.

2. To assemble the sandwiches, spread 4 slices of bread with the mayonnaise and top with the turkey. Spread the remaining 4 slices of bread with cranberry sauce and set them on top of the turkey.

3. Slice the sandwiches in half and serve.

CRANBERRY SAUCE

Makes 1¼ cups

¾ cup fresh cranberries

2 tablespoons sugar

½ cup water

2 teaspoons grated orange zest

1. In a medium saucepan over medium heat, combine the cranberries, sugar, and water. Bring to a boil and whisk to break up the cranberries.

2. Cook the mixture until the cranberries burst and the sauce has thickened, about 5 minutes. Remove from the heat and stir in the zest.

3. Cool completely before serving, or store in the refrigerator in an airtight container.

Kitchen Vocabulary

Zest is the outer part of the peel of any citrus fruit (each has its own distinct flavor). You can remove it in light flakes using a kitchen rasp (Microplane is a common brand name) or in larger pieces using a vegetable peeler; mince the larger pieces before using. Just make sure you only remove the colorful outer layer and none of the inner white layer (the pith), which tastes bitter.

OPEN-FACED MUSHROOM TORTAS

Makes 10 servings

Quick Pickled Onions

1 cup white vinegar

1 tablespoon salt

1 tablespoon sugar

1¾ cups thinly sliced red onion

Mushroom Filling

1½ tablespoons olive oil

2 cups minced white onion

5 cloves garlic, minced

4 cups thinly sliced button mushrooms

1 jalapeño, seeds removed and thinly sliced
(optional)

¼ cup lime juice

2 teaspoons salt

1¼ cups Refried Beans (page 132)

5 Kaiser rolls, cut in half lengthwise

2 avocados, sliced

½ cup crumbled queso fresco cheese
(see Chef's Notes)

1. To make the pickled onions, place the vinegar, salt, and sugar in a small saucepan over medium heat. Cook until the sugar and salt dissolve, about 4 minutes.

2. Place the onions in a medium-sized jar or heat-resistant bowl and add the vinegar mixture. Cover and refrigerate until needed, at least 1 hour.

3. To make the mushroom filling, heat the oil in a medium sauté pan over medium heat. Add the onions and garlic and cook, stirring with a wooden spoon, until the onions begin to soften, about 4 minutes. Add the mushrooms and jalapeño, if using, and cook, stirring, until the mushrooms have softened and are beginning to brown around the edges, about 5 minutes.

4. Add the lime juice and salt and cook until the lime juice evaporates and the pan is dry, about 4 minutes. Remove from the heat and let cool before using.

5. To assemble the sandwiches, spread about 2 tablespoons refried beans on each half of a roll. Top each roll half with ½ cup of mushroom filling, then finish with the avocado, pickled onions, and cheese.

Chef's Notes

A torta is a Mexican sandwich.

The mushroom filling can also be used in tacos, quesadillas, and burritos.

Queso fresco means "fresh cheese" in Spanish. This is a common Mexican cheese that melts well and has a mild flavor.

ROASTED VEGETABLE BOWLS

Makes 5 servings

Roasted Squash

1¾ cups (about 8 ounces) diced butternut squash

1¾ cups (about 8 ounces) diced acorn squash

4 tablespoons olive oil

Farro

3 tablespoons olive oil

3 tablespoons minced onion

2 cups uncooked farro

4 cups water

1 tablespoon olive oil

2 cups chopped green cabbage

½ cup chopped parsley

1. To make the roasted squash, preheat the oven to 450°F.

2. In a medium bowl, toss the butternut squash and acorn squash with the oil. Transfer to an aluminum foil–lined baking sheet and roast until the squash is brown around the edges and completely cooked, about 1 hour. Remove from the oven and set aside while you make the farro.

3. Meanwhile, to make the farro, in a medium saucepan, heat the oil over medium heat. Add the onion and cook, stirring with a wooden spoon, until the onion has softened and is fragrant, about 2 minutes. Add the farro and cook for about 2 more minutes.

4. Add the water and bring the mixture to a simmer over medium heat. Reduce the heat, cover the pan, and simmer until the farro is cooked and the water is absorbed, about 25 minutes.

5. While the farro is cooking, heat the oil in a large pan over medium heat. Add the cabbage and cook, stirring, until it is softened and browning around the edges, about 5 minutes.

6. Transfer the cabbage to a large bowl and mix it with the cooked farro and squash. Stir in the parsley and serve immediately.

Using Fresh Herbs

Fresh herbs are best when used at the end of cooking, to finish a dish—like adding thyme just before a soup is done or sprinkling ribbons of basil over the top of a pizza. This way the flavors are still fresh for serving. Fresh herbs work well in sauces, salad dressings, and other quick dishes since dried herbs don't have enough time to really infuse these kinds of dishes.

FARRO CAPRESE SALAD

Makes 5 servings

- 2 cups cooked farro, cooled (see Chef's Note)
- 1 cup diced mozzarella cheese
- 1 cup grape tomatoes, halved
- ½ cup yellow pear tomatoes, halved
- ½ cup coarsely chopped fresh basil
- 3 tablespoons extra-virgin olive oil
- 1 tablespoon balsamic vinegar
- 1 teaspoon salt

1. In a medium bowl, combine the farro, cheese, grape tomatoes, yellow pear tomatoes, and basil. Add the oil, vinegar, and salt, and mix to combine.

2. Cover and refrigerate until ready to serve.

Chef's Note

Farro is a whole grain that is rich in protein and fiber. It has a slightly chewy bite and a nutty whole-grain flavor.

Cooking Farro

To cook farro: Place 1 cup farro in a pot and add ½ teaspoon salt and 2 cups water. Bring to a boil over medium heat. Reduce to a simmer, cover, and cook for 20 to 25 minutes, or until the farro has absorbed all the liquid. 1 cup dry farro = 2 cups cooked

MAIN MEALS FOR LUNCH AND DINNER

Asian-Style Baked Chicken

Baked Honey Mustard Pork or Chicken

Oven "Barbequed" Chicken

Oven Barbequed Baby Back Ribs

Tomato and Cheese Quesadillas

Meatless Lasagna

Ratatouille

Stuffed Shells

Chicken Parmesan

Chicken Curry

Pizza

Nachos Supreme

Tex-Mex Chicken and Cheese
Toasted Burritos

Tacos

Turkey Meatballs

Crispy Cracker-Coated Fish

Pan-Fried Shrimp

Fried Rice

Shrimp Potstickers

Chinese Take-Out Chicken and Broccoli

Cheeseburgers

Quick and Easy Macaroni and Cheese

Ramen Noodle Stir Fry

Beef or Chicken Satay with Peanut Sauce

BBQ Grilled Chicken

ASIAN-STYLE BAKED CHICKEN

Makes 6 to 8 servings

3 tablespoons soy sauce

2 tablespoons rice vinegar or cider vinegar

2 tablespoons water

2 tablespoons light brown sugar

1 tablespoon sesame seeds

1 tablespoon vegetable oil

2 teaspoons sesame oil

1½ teaspoons garlic powder

2 pounds chicken breast or thighs

1. In a small bowl, combine the soy sauce, vinegar, water, brown sugar, sesame seeds, vegetable oil, sesame oil, and garlic powder to make a marinade.

2. Place the chicken in a large resealable storage bag or medium-sized container. Pour the sesame marinade over the chicken and place in the refrigerator, sealed or covered, for at least 2 hours or up to overnight.

3. Preheat the oven to 375°F and line a rimmed baking sheet with foil.

4. Place the marinated chicken on the prepared baking sheet.

5. Bake for 30 to 45 minutes, or until the juices from the chicken run clear when you pierce it with a knife and it reaches an internal temperature of 165°F.

Kitchen Vocabulary

A **marinade** is a flavorful liquid mix that typically contains seasonings, oil, and an acidic ingredient like citrus juice or vinegar, in which meat, vegetables, tofu, fish, or other ingredients are soaked before cooking in order to add flavor and sometimes to tenderize.

BAKED HONEY MUSTARD PORK OR CHICKEN

Makes 6 to 8 servings

¼ cup yellow mustard

2 tablespoons honey

2 tablespoons Texas-Style BBQ Sauce (page 145), or your favorite store-bought variety

1½ teaspoons salt

1 teaspoon lemon juice

½ teaspoon curry powder

½ teaspoon sugar

2 pounds boneless pork loin or chicken breast

1. Preheat the oven to 350°F and line a 9-by-9-inch baking dish with aluminum foil.

2. In a large bowl, combine the mustard, honey, barbeque sauce, salt, lemon juice, curry powder, and sugar, and mix to combine. Add the pork or chicken and rub the sauce into the meat until it is coated.

3. Place the pork or chicken into the prepared baking dish and pour the remaining sauce over the meat.

4. Bake for 30 to 45 minutes, or until the juices from the meat run clear when you pierce it with a knife and it reaches an internal temperature of 150°F for pork or 165°F for chicken.

5. Remove from the oven. Let the meat stand for about 5 minutes, then slice and serve.

OVEN "BARBEQUED" CHICKEN

Makes 6 to 8 servings

> 3 pounds chicken quarters
>
> ½ cup Texas-Style BBQ Sauce (page 145), or your favorite store-bought variety
>
> ¼ cup water
>
> 4 teaspoons Spice Rub for Meat (page 122)
>
> ½ teaspoon salt

1. Place the chicken in a large bowl and mix in the barbeque sauce, water, spice rub, and salt to make a marinade. Cover the bowl and refrigerate for 3 hours.

2. Preheat the oven to 350°F and line a rimmed baking sheet with aluminum foil.

3. Transfer the chicken pieces to the baking sheet. Pour the remaining marinade over the chicken.

4. Bake for 45 minutes to 1 hour, until the juices from the chicken run clear when you pierce it with a knife and it reaches an internal temperature of 165°F.

OVEN BARBEQUED BABY BACK RIBS

Makes 8 to 10 servings

> 4 teaspoons Spice Rub for Meat (page 122)
>
> 2 pounds pork spare ribs
>
> ½ cup Texas-Style BBQ Sauce (page 145), or your favorite store-bought variety
>
> ½ cup water

1. Preheat the oven to 325°F and line a rimmed baking sheet with aluminum foil.

2. Evenly sprinkle the spice rub over both sides of the ribs and place them on the baking sheet.

3. In a small bowl, combine the barbeque sauce and water, then pour over the ribs, evenly coating them.

4. Cover the baking sheet with foil and bake for 1½ hours.

5. Remove the foil and bake for about 1 hour more, until the meat easily separates from the bone with a fork and the sauce is thickened.

6. Cut the ribs into 1- or 2-bone pieces. Toss the ribs in the sauce before serving.

TOMATO AND CHEESE QUESADILLAS

Makes four 8-inch quesadillas (4 servings)

1 cup chopped tomato

1 teaspoon garlic powder

½ teaspoon salt

Pinch of ground black pepper

Pinch of dried oregano

Eight 8-inch flour tortillas

1½ cups shredded cheddar or Monterey Jack cheese

1. Preheat the oven to 300°F.

2. Combine the tomato, garlic powder, salt, pepper, and oregano in a small bowl.

3. Place 4 tortillas on a rimmed baking sheet and top each with an equal amount of the tomato mixture, then top with the shredded cheese.

4. Place another tortilla on top of each quesadilla and press down with your hand.

5. Cook for 5 to 10 minutes or until the cheese is melted.

6. Cut each quesadilla into 4 or 6 wedges and serve.

Think Like a Chef

Quesadillas are sort of like grilled cheese in a tortilla, so the same rules apply: Use cheeses that get really melty, and add other ingredients that are on the soft side, or already cooked. Leftovers are a great source—cooked beans, meats, and vegetables are all fair game.

Chicken Fajita Quesadillas: sautéed onions + sautéed peppers + grilled chicken + guacamole + sour cream

BBQ Pork Quesadillas: barbeque pulled pork + red onion

Spinach and Mushroom Quesadillas: sautéed mushrooms + garlic + spinach + lemon juice

Spicy Shrimp and Corn Quesadillas: cooked shrimp + corn + roasted chiles + hot sauce

MEATLESS LASAGNA

Makes 6 to 8 servings

1 pound lasagna noodles

15 ounces (about 3 cups) Ricotta Cheese (page 97; double the recipe), or store-bought

¼ teaspoon ground black pepper

¼ teaspoon ground nutmeg

6 cups Grandma's Tomato Sauce (page 141)

1 pound (4 cups) shredded mozzarella cheese

1. Preheat the oven to 350°F.

2. Bring a large pot of salted water to a boil over high heat. Add the lasagna noodles and stir gently as they soften in the boiling water to make sure they don't stick together. Cook the noodles until they are just barely tender, about 8 minutes. Drain in a colander and set aside.

3. In a medium bowl, combine the ricotta, pepper, and nutmeg.

4. Spread 1 cup of the tomato sauce evenly onto the bottom of a 9-by-13-inch baking pan.

5. Lay out an even layer of lasagna noodles on top of the sauce.

6. Cover the lasagna noodles with another 1 cup of tomato sauce, then ¾ cup of the mozzarella, and about ½ cup of the ricotta mixture in evenly dispersed dollops.

7. Repeat this layering process until all of the lasagna noodles have been used.

8. Top the last layer of lasagna noodles with the remaining sauce and the remaining mozzarella.

9. Bake for 30 to 40 minutes, until the cheese is melted and the lasagna is very hot and bubbling.

RATATOUILLE

Makes 6 servings

1 tablespoon olive oil

2 cups chopped bell peppers, any color

2 cups chopped eggplant

1½ cups chopped onion

1 tablespoon chopped garlic

1½ cups chopped tomatoes

1 cup chopped zucchini

1 cup chopped yellow squash

1 teaspoon salt

½ teaspoon minced thyme

½ teaspoon minced oregano

½ teaspoon ground black pepper

½ teaspoon sugar

1. Heat the oil in a large pot or sauté pan over medium heat. Add the peppers, eggplant, and onions and cook, stirring with a wooden spoon, for about 5 minutes. Add the garlic and stir.

2. Add the tomatoes, zucchini, yellow squash, salt, thyme, oregano, pepper, and sugar.

3. Cook, stirring, until all the vegetables are tender and fully cooked, 10 to 20 minutes.

Chef's Note

You can substitute canned tomatoes or tomato sauce for the fresh tomatoes.

STUFFED SHELLS

Makes 6 servings

1 box (12 to 16 ounces) large pasta shells

1 pound (about 4 cups) shredded mozzarella cheese

1½ cups Ricotta Cheese (recipe follows), or store bought

½ cup grated Parmesan cheese

1 egg

1½ teaspoons salt

½ teaspoon dried oregano

⅛ teaspoon ground black pepper

3 cups Grandma's Tomato Sauce (page 141)

1. Preheat the oven to 350°F.

2. Bring a large pot of salted water to a boil over high heat. Add the pasta shells and stir gently as they soften in the boiling water to make sure they don't stick together. Cook the shells until they are just barely tender, about 8 minutes. Drain in a colander and set aside.

3. In a medium bowl, combine half the mozzarella and the ricotta, Parmesan, egg, salt, oregano, and pepper. Transfer the filling to a piping bag (see Chef's Note). (You could also use a zip-top bag if you don't have a piping bag; cut one corner off the bag.)

4. Pour 1 cup of the tomato sauce into the bottom of a 9-by-13-inch baking pan.

5. Squeeze the filling out of the hole in the bag to pipe about 1 tablespoon of filling into each shell, then arrange the shells in the pan in rows.

6. Pour the remaining sauce over the shells and top with the rest of the mozzarella.

7. Bake for 35 minutes, until the cheese is melted and the filling is very hot.

Chef's Note

A piping bag is a cone-shaped bag, made from disposable plastic or reusable cloth, that is used to portion out soft or liquid foods such as this ricotta cheese filling, deviled egg filling, cookie dough, or frosting (it is often used for cake decorating). A hole is cut at the pointy end of the bag and the food is squeezed out through the hole. Piping bags can be fitted with metal tips to make decorative shapes, such as flat lines, star shapes, or rounded edges.

RICOTTA CHEESE

Makes 1½ cups

2 quarts whole milk

3 tablespoons white vinegar

1. Pour the milk into a medium saucepan and bring it to a simmer over medium heat, stirring occasionally so that it doesn't burn.

2. Once the milk has come to a simmer, turn off the heat and slowly stir in the vinegar until the curds and whey separate.

3. Place a fine mesh strainer over a bowl. Use a slotted spoon to lift the cheese curds out of the pot and transfer to the strainer, then allow them to drain for at least 1 hour.

4. Refrigerate the ricotta in a covered container until ready to use.

DIY

Making cheese at home is easier than you think and worth every minute! Fresh, homemade cheese is creamy and flavorful, and this two-ingredient Ricotta Cheese is perfect for use in Stuffed Shells, on Pizza (page 100), or in Meatless Lasagna (page 95).

Chef's Notes

When making cheese, the lumpy, solid bits that form are called curds, and the remaining liquid is called whey. When the vinegar (or any acidic ingredient) is added to the milk, it causes the milk proteins to separate into curds and whey. When making harder cheeses, like Swiss or cheddar, the whey is drained and the curds are pressed until they come together to form a solid block of cheese.

The finished cheese can be seasoned with salt, pepper, or fresh herbs, or eaten sweet with fruit and honey. To make it creamier, stir in 1 to 2 tablespoons of milk or cream.

CHICKEN PARMESAN

Makes 4 to 6 servings

3 boneless, skinless chicken breasts

½ teaspoon salt

Pinch of ground black pepper

½ cup all-purpose flour

2 eggs

1 tablespoon water

1¾ cups bread crumbs

¼ cup canola oil

3 cups Grandma's Tomato Sauce (page 141)

8 ounces (about 1½ cups) shredded mozzarella cheese

1. Preheat the oven to 350°F, with a rack near the top of the oven.

2. Cut the chicken breasts in half lengthwise, as if you were cutting a sub roll. You will have 6 thin pieces. Season the chicken with the salt and pepper.

3. Place the flour in a medium bowl. Mix the eggs and water together in a separate bowl. Place the bread crumbs in another bowl. Place all three bowls on the counter side by side.

4. Coat each piece of chicken in the flour first, then dip it into the eggs, and finally into the bread crumbs, pressing the bread crumbs into the chicken so they adhere.

5. Heat the oil in a large sauté pan over medium heat. Once the oil is hot, carefully add the breaded chicken. Cook over medium heat until one side is golden brown, about 4 minutes. Turn the chicken over using a fork or a pair of tongs and cook until the other side is golden brown, the juices run clear when you pierce it with a knife, and the chicken has reached an internal temperature of 165°F.

6. In a small saucepan, heat the tomato sauce to a simmer over medium heat. Pour half the sauce into a casserole dish large enough to hold all of the chicken. Place the chicken on top of the sauce and then pour the rest of the sauce over the chicken. Top with the shredded cheese. Bake on the top rack of the oven for 15 to 20 minutes, until the cheese has melted.

Variation

EGGPLANT PARMESAN

Substitute 1 large eggplant, cut into ¼-inch slices, for the chicken to make Eggplant Parmesan. Follow the directions as written, cooking the eggplant until it is golden brown on each side in Step 5.

CHICKEN CURRY

Makes 6 servings

2 tablespoons vegetable oil

1 cup chopped onions

½ cup chopped carrots

2 tablespoons minced fresh ginger

2 tablespoons chopped garlic

4 tablespoons all-purpose flour

2 teaspoons sugar

1 to 2 teaspoons curry powder (depending on how spicy you like it)

1½ teaspoons salt

⅛ teaspoon ground black pepper

2¾ cups chicken stock

1 pound boneless skinless chicken breast, cut into cubes

1. Heat the oil in a medium saucepan over medium heat.

2. Add the onions, carrots, ginger, and garlic and cook, stirring with a wooden spoon, until the vegetables begin to soften, about 5 minutes.

3. Reduce the heat to low, stir in the flour, sugar, curry powder, salt, and pepper, and cook for 1 minute.

4. Pour in the chicken stock, whisking to avoid lumps. Increase the heat to medium, and simmer for about 15 minutes.

5. Add the chicken and cook until it is fully cooked, about 15 minutes more. Serve immediately.

Chef's Notes

Serve chicken curry over cooked white rice with Naan-Style Flatbread (page 140) on the side.

Curry powder is a combination of dried spices that is frequently used in South Asian cooking. There are many varieties of curry and the ingredients vary depending on the region. Indian-style curry powders typically contain coriander, turmeric, cumin, and chili powder, but might also be flavored with cinnamon, cardamom, clove, and mustard. You can make your own curry powder by experimenting with these spices in combinations that you enjoy!

Cooking Rice

To cook long-grain white rice: Place 1 cup rice in a pot and add 2 cups water. Bring to a boil over medium heat. Reduce to a simmer, cover, and cook for 20 to 25 minutes, or until the rice has absorbed all the liquid. **To cook short-grain white rice:** follow the same procedure, using 1¼ cups water for 1 cup rice.

PIZZA

Makes two 12- to 14-inch pizzas (6 to 8 servings)

Dough

2 cups warm water

1 tablespoon extra-virgin olive oil, plus more as needed

2 teaspoons instant yeast

1 teaspoon sugar

4¼ cups all-purpose flour, plus more for dusting

1 teaspoon salt

Quick Pizza Sauce (recipe follows)

Any toppings you like (see page 103)

1. To make the dough, in the bowl of a stand mixer, stir together the water, oil, yeast, and sugar.

2. Place the dough hook onto the mixer and add the flour to the bowl. Add the salt.

3. Mix on low speed until the dough is smooth, about 5 minutes.

4. Remove the bowl from the mixer and brush the top of the dough with oil. Cover the bowl with plastic wrap and let rise in a warm place for about 45 minutes.

5. Dust a clean surface with flour and remove the dough from the bowl.

6. Pizza bakes best in a hot oven, so preheat your oven to 450°F. You can bake your pizza either on a baking sheet dusted with flour or fine cornmeal or on a pizza stone, if you have one. If using a pizza stone, put it in the oven to preheat.

7. Cut the dough into two pieces. Roll the dough into two round ball shapes and cover them with the plastic wrap. Let the dough rest for 15 to 20 minutes.

8. Dust each ball with flour and, using a rolling pin or your hands, form each ball of dough into a round pizza shape, as thick or thin as you like it.

9. Set each pizza on a baking sheet or on a floured pizza peel if you are using a pizza stone. Add sauce and whatever toppings you like.

10. Transfer the pizzas to the oven and bake until the edges and bottoms are golden brown and the cheese is melted and bubbly, about 30 minutes.

Chef's Note

After resting, the dough can be shaped using your hands or a rolling pin. If it gets overworked, it will tighten and be hard to shape. If the dough becomes hard to work with, put it aside to rest for about 30 minutes before continuing to shape.

QUICK PIZZA SAUCE

Makes about 3½ cups

One 28-ounce can whole tomatoes

2 tablespoons Parmesan cheese

2 cloves garlic

1 teaspoon sugar

1 teaspoon dried oregano

¼ teaspoon salt

Combine the tomatoes, cheese, garlic, sugar, oregano, and salt in a blender and process until smooth, about 1 minute. You'll need about ¾ cup of sauce for each pizza. Extra sauce can be simmered for 30 minutes to thicken and then stored in an airtight container in the refrigerator.

Continued

Chef's Note

How much sauce and cheese do I need?

- Each 12- to 14-inch pizza will use about ¾ cup of sauce.
- Each 12- to 14-inch pizza will use ½ pound of shredded cheese.

Pour the sauce in the middle of the pizza and, using the bottom of a ladle, move the sauce around in a circular motion. This technique ensures that the center of the pie is not too heavy and saturated with sauce.

Gear Up

Pizza stones are available in home goods and kitchenware stores. To use one, place it in the oven as soon as you turn it on. Once the pizza dough is stretched out, place the pizza on a floured pizza peel (a wooden board used to transfer pizza to and from the oven) and add the sauce and toppings, then carefully use the peel to transfer the pizza onto the pizza stone in the oven. If you don't have a pizza peel, you can use the floured back of a baking sheet to transfer the pizza to the oven.

If you don't have a pizza stone, you can stretch or roll the dough and place it on a baking sheet lightly dusted with flour, cornmeal, or semolina flour.

Variation
CALZONE

A calzone is like a large turnover. Roll the dough out to ¼ inch thick and place it on a cookie sheet. Arrange the sauce, cheese, and toppings on half of the dough. Fold the other half of the dough over, making sure to force out the air, and then pinch the edges to seal everything inside. Bake the calzone until it is golden brown.

Chef's Note

Keep it simple: If you pile on too many toppings, it will be much harder to get the pizza in and out of the oven.

Toppings

Cheese: Mozzarella can be purchased in 1-pound blocks or shredded and is the traditional cheese for pizza. Other varieties that work well are Parmesan, provolone, or ricotta, but you can experiment with any of your favorite cheeses.

Onions, garlic, and peppers: Slice thin and use raw or sautéed. Don't brown the garlic when sautéing or it will taste bitter.

Mushrooms: Slice fresh mushrooms and sauté in a little olive oil or butter before adding to the pizza.

Meatballs: Use whole or sliced cooked meatballs.

Pepperoni: Can be purchased in the deli section of the supermarket.

Ham: Chopped or torn deli ham tastes great paired with pineapple for a Hawaiian pizza.

Did You Know?

In the United States, pepperoni is the most popular of all the pizza toppings.

NACHOS SUPREME

Makes 4 to 6 servings

1½ cups Refried Beans (page 132), hot
1 medium bag (6 to 9 ounces) tortilla chips
1½ cups shredded cheddar cheese
1 cup chopped fresh tomatoes
½ cup Tomato Salsa (page 156) or Green Tomatillo Salsa (page 157)
1 cup Guacamole (page 154)

1. Preheat the oven to 350°F.

2. Using a spoon or butter knife, spread the refried beans in the middle of an oven-safe platter or baking sheet. Arrange the tortilla chips on top of and around the beans. Sprinkle the cheese evenly over the chips and beans.

3. Place the nachos in the oven and bake for 8 to 10 minutes, until the cheese is melted.

4. Remove from the oven and top with the tomatoes, salsa, and guacamole.

Chef's Note

You can add many different toppings to nachos to make them extra supreme, including cooked chicken, black beans, jalapeño slices, corn, or chopped bell peppers.

TEX-MEX CHICKEN AND CHEESE TOASTED BURRITOS

Makes 6 burritos (6 servings)

1 cooked rotisserie chicken (12 to 14 ounces of meat)

2 cups shredded cheddar or Monterey Jack cheese

¾ cup Tomato Salsa (page 156)

½ cup sour cream

6 flour tortillas (8 or 10 inches in diameter)

1 tablespoon butter

1 tablespoon vegetable oil

1. Remove all of the meat from the chicken and shred or chop it. Combine the chicken with the cheese, salsa, and sour cream in a medium bowl.

2. Lay the tortillas on a baking sheet and divide the filling among them, placing it in the center of each tortilla. For each tortilla, fold the edge closest to you over the filling, then fold the left and right sides over and roll into a burrito. (If the tortillas are firm and difficult to fold, it might be helpful to warm them slightly in the oven or a microwave before you add the filling.)

3. Heat a large sauté pan over medium heat and add the butter and oil. Add the burritos, with the seam side down on the pan. Cook, flipping the burritos as needed, until they are golden brown on both sides and the cheese is melted, about 5 minutes.

Think Like a Chef

You can wrap the components of any favorite meal in a flour tortilla. Heating it in a pan makes the outside crisp and the inside warm and melty — soooo good.

Thai-Style Chicken Burrito
chicken + brown rice + cabbage + mango + peanuts + peanut sauce (page 120)

Mediterranean Veggie Burrito
chickpeas + garlic + tomato + spinach + feta cheese + lemon juice

Spicy Breakfast Burrito
scrambled eggs + bell pepper + crispy bacon + cheddar cheese + pickled jalapeños + hot sauce

Curry Burrito
potatoes + peas + carrots + curry powder + paneer + yogurt

TACOS

Makes 8 tacos (4 servings)

2 tablespoons vegetable oil

1¼ pounds ground beef, turkey, pork, or chicken

¼ cup Texas-Style BBQ Sauce (page 145)

2 tablespoons water

4 teaspoons Spice Rub for Meat (page 122)

8 taco shells

1 cup diced tomato

1 cup shredded lettuce

½ cup shredded cheese

1. Heat the oil in a large sauté pan over medium heat. Add the ground meat and cook, stirring, until it is browned and fully cooked, about 7 minutes.

2. Add the barbeque sauce, water, and spice rub.

3. Bring the mixture to a simmer and cook until it thickens slightly, about 3 minutes.

4. Serve the tacos buffet-style with the meat, taco shells, tomatoes, lettuce, and cheese.

Chef's Note

This meat mixture is also delicious when served as Sloppy Joes or in burritos.

Which Tortillas?

You can use any kind of tortilla you like to make tacos, whether soft or crunchy. Tortillas come in either corn or flour varieties, but can also include other ingredients like spinach and sun-dried tomatoes, or can be white or whole wheat. Choose which one to use depending on what is going inside your tacos, or use more than one kind.

Think Like a Chef

Be creative with your tacos, but remember that they are thought of as a lighter, fresher cousin to the burrito, so don't add ingredients that are too heavy or filling.

Fish Tacos: flaky white fish + red cabbage + sour cream + chipotle sauce + flour tortillas

Tempeh Tacos: grilled tempeh + hummus + cucumber + lemon juice + parsley

Steak Tacos: steak + Quick Pickled Onions (page 87) + lime juice + cilantro + cotija cheese

Black Bean Tacos: black beans + corn + avocado + lime juice + cilantro + corn tortillas

What Is Cotija?

Cotija is a hard cow's milk cheese from Mexico. It is named after the town of Cotija in the state of Michoacán. El queso Cotija de Montaña, or "grain cheese," is dry and firm, with little taste other than saltiness. You can use Parmesan cheese in place of cotija.

TURKEY MEATBALLS

Makes about 12 meatballs

2 teaspoons olive oil

1 cup chopped onion

½ cup chopped celery

2 teaspoons garlic powder

1¼ pounds ground turkey (see Chef's Notes)

¾ cup bread crumbs

¼ cup ketchup

¼ cup grated Parmesan cheese

2 eggs

3 tablespoons chopped parsley

2 teaspoons dried oregano

1½ teaspoons salt

½ teaspoon ground black pepper

1. Preheat the oven to 400°F.

2. Heat the oil in a sauté pan over medium heat. Add the onion, celery, and garlic powder. Cook, stirring with a wooden spoon, until the vegetables are softened, about 5 minutes.

3. Transfer the vegetables to a medium mixing bowl.

4. Add the turkey, bread crumbs, ketchup, cheese, eggs, parsley, oregano, salt, and pepper to the vegetable mixture. Mix with a wooden spoon until the ingredients are well incorporated.

5. Roll the mixture into 12 equal balls and place in a lightly-oiled casserole dish or baking sheet.

6. Bake until the meatballs are golden brown and a meat thermometer registers 165°F when inserted in the center of a meatball, 15 to 20 minutes.

Think Like a Chef

You can change these to fit any of your favorite flavor profiles by using different ground meats and seasonings. Serve them as a side dish with a salad for lunch, add them to spaghetti with Grandma's Tomato Sauce (page 141), or make them into a traditional Italian meatball hero sandwich.

Mediterranean Lamb Meatballs: ground lamb + garlic + cumin + mint

Swedish Meatballs: ground beef + mushrooms + dried onion flakes

Chef's Notes

You could use other ground meats, like beef, pork, or lamb, to make these meatballs. You can even combine more than one type of meat, like beef and pork, which is very common in Italian-style meatballs.

In this recipe, the bread crumbs and eggs act as binders. This means that they act like glue to hold all of the other ingredients together in the meatball shape.

CRISPY CRACKER-COATED FISH

Makes 4 servings

1 pound white fish, such as flounder or tilapia

½ teaspoon salt

⅛ teaspoon ground black pepper

Cracker Coating

1 cup crushed crackers, any kind

¼ cup Panko bread crumbs

½ cup plus 3 tablespoons all-purpose flour

½ teaspoon paprika

⅛ teaspoon garlic powder

2 eggs

¼ cup vegetable oil

1. Cut the fish into 4 equal portions and season with the salt and pepper.

2. To make the cracker coating, place the crushed crackers, bread crumbs, 3 tablespoons of the flour, the paprika, and garlic powder in a zip-top bag. Crush the cracker mixture with a rolling pin or your fist.

3. Place the remaining ½ cup flour in a wide, shallow bowl. Beat the eggs together in a separate bowl. Place the cracker mixture in another bowl, and place all three bowls on the counter side by side.

4. Coat each piece of fish in the flour, then dip it in the eggs, and finally in the cracker crumbs, pressing the cracker crumbs into the fish so they adhere.

5. Heat the oil in a large sauté pan over medium heat. Once the oil is hot, carefully add the breaded fish.

6. Cook over medium heat until golden brown on one side, about 4 minutes. Turn the fish over using a fork or pair of tongs and cook until golden brown on the other side and the fish has reached an internal temperature of 145°F. Serve immediately.

PAN-FRIED SHRIMP

Makes 4 to 6 servings

| 1 pound peeled and deveined medium shrimp |
| 1 tablespoon lemon juice |
| ½ teaspoon salt |
| ¼ teaspoon ground black pepper |
| 2½ cups panko bread crumbs |
| ½ cup all-purpose flour |
| 3 eggs |
| 6 tablespoons vegetable oil |

1. In a large bowl, combine the shrimp with the lemon juice, salt, and pepper to season.

2. Place the bread crumbs, flour, and eggs in three separate bowls, and set them on the counter side by side. Beat the eggs. Coat each shrimp in the flour, then dip it into the beaten eggs, and then in the bread crumbs, pressing the bread crumbs into the shrimp until they are well coated.

3. Heat the oil in a large sauté pan over medium heat. In batches, being careful not to crowd the pan, add the shrimp and cook, flipping once, until golden brown on the outside and white in the center, about 2 minutes per side.

4. Transfer the finished shrimp to a paper-towel-lined plate. Serve while still warm.

Chef's Note

When pan frying, it is very important not to crowd the pan. This means that the pieces of food shouldn't be too close together or touching each other. When there is too much in the pan, the heat and steam build up around the food, which makes it soggy instead of crispy and golden brown. If you have more pieces than can fit in the pan with room in between, fry your food in batches, one after another.

Think Like a Chef

You can eat these fried shrimp plain or with tartar sauce, which is a very common accompaniment. But there are lots of other ways to serve them! Make a New Orleans-style po'boy sandwich with lettuce, tomato, and some spicy mayonnaise. Or add the shrimp to a raw spinach salad for some crunch! You could even top them with Grandma's Tomato Sauce (page 141) and some mozzarella cheese to make shrimp parmesan.

Peeled and Deveined

Deveined means the long vein that runs down the length of the shrimp has been removed. You can buy shrimp already peeled and deveined at the grocery store.

What Size Shrimp?

Shrimp are sized according to their "count," meaning how many shrimp there are per pound. The smaller the number is, the larger the shrimp, and the larger the number, the smaller the shrimp. A count of 21/25 means that there are an average of 21 to 25 shrimp per pound. For medium-sized shrimp, look for a count of 36/40.

FRIED RICE

Makes about 4 cups (4 servings)

- 2 tablespoons vegetable oil
- ½ cup chopped onion
- ½ cup sliced green onions
- 1 tablespoon finely chopped garlic
- 1 tablespoon minced fresh ginger
- ¼ cup chopped deli-style ham
- 3 cups cooked rice, cold
- 3 tablespoons soy sauce

1. Heat the oil in a wok or large sauté pan over high heat. Add the onion, green onion, garlic, and ginger to the pan and cook, stirring constantly, until fragrant, about 30 seconds.

2. Add the ham and rice and cook, stirring constantly, until the rice is hot, about 3 minutes.

3. Add the soy sauce and stir to incorporate. Serve hot.

Use Leftover Rice

It's best to use leftover rice that has been cooked and refrigerated when making fried rice. If the rice is just cooked or not cold, its starch is too easily released and you will end up with a sticky, gummy mess.

Try Other Grains in Place of Rice

You can fry other grains besides rice to add some new flavors and textures to your dish. Cooked barley, brown rice, farro, quinoa, and wild rice offer great flavors and textures (although quinoa is not technically a grain but a different type of seed).

Did You Know?

Rice is a grain that is produced on every continent except Antarctica and is a symbol of life and fertility in many cultures. It's an important world crop, supplying about 25% of the world's per-capita calories. The average American eats about 25 pounds of rice per year, which equals about 725,000 individual grains.

Think Like a Chef

You can add lots of other ingredients to fried rice. Just be sure to use roughly the same amounts as in the recipe here.

Spicy Kimchi Fried Rice: prepared kimchi + scallions + fried egg

Pineapple Fried Rice: pineapple + shrimp + scallions + cilantro

Cajun Fried Rice: Andouille sausage + shrimp + bell pepper + onion + paprika + dried thyme

Fall Farro Fried Rice: butternut squash + parsnips + green cabbage + pumpkin seeds (use cooked farro instead of rice)

SHRIMP POTSTICKERS

Makes 16 potstickers (4 servings)

Filling

4 ounces peeled and deveined medium shrimp, chopped

4 cups shredded Napa cabbage

½ cup minced scallions

1 tablespoon minced fresh ginger

1 tablespoon minced garlic

2 teaspoons sugar

2 teaspoons soy sauce

1 teaspoon sesame oil

½ teaspoon salt

¼ teaspoon ground black pepper

1 tablespoon vegetable oil, plus more for frying

1 cup plus 1 tablespoon water

2 tablespoons all-purpose flour

16 round dumpling wrappers (see Chef's Notes)

1. To make the filling, in a large mixing bowl, combine the shrimp, cabbage, scallions, ginger, garlic, sugar, soy sauce, sesame oil, salt, and pepper.

2. Heat the oil in a large sauté pan over medium heat. Add the filling mixture and cook, stirring occasionally, until the cabbage has cooked down and is soft, about 10 minutes. Transfer the filling from the pan to a large bowl and let cool completely.

3. In a small bowl, combine 1 tablespoon of the water and the flour to form a paste.

4. Lay the dumpling wrappers on a work surface and use your finger or a pastry brush to brush the edges with the flour paste.

5. Place 1 tablespoon of the cooled filling in the center of each dumpling wrapper. Fold the wrapper over the filling and seal it by pressing the tines of a fork along the edge of the dumpling.

6. To cook the dumplings, heat about 3 tablespoons of oil in a large sauté pan over medium heat. Lay the dumplings in a single layer, flat side down, in the pan, making sure the entire bottom of the pan is covered. Cook until the dumplings are golden brown on the bottom, 1 to 3 minutes.

7. Reduce the heat to low, carefully pour the remaining 1 cup of water into the pan, and then cover with a lid or aluminum foil. Turn the heat back to medium and cook until the dumplings are fully cooked and very hot, about 5 minutes. Serve immediately, with Potsticker Dipping Sauce (recipe follows) on the side.

POTSTICKER DIPPING SAUCE

Makes ½ cup

¼ cup soy sauce

2 tablespoons rice wine vinegar

½ teaspoon sesame oil

½ teaspoon grated fresh ginger

2 tablespoons thinly sliced scallions

In a small bowl, combine the soy sauce, vinegar, sesame oil, ginger, and scallions. Refrigerate until ready to use.

crispy side

Chef's Notes

You can substitute ground beef, turkey, or pork for the shrimp.

Dumpling wrappers are available in the frozen section of most grocery stores and Asian markets.

About Potstickers

Potstickers are thinly wrapped Asian dumplings filled with ground meats, seafood, and/or vegetables that are pan fried until crispy on one side and then steamed. They are always served with a soy-based dipping sauce, which can be sweet, salty, sour, and even spicy.

CHINESE TAKE-OUT CHICKEN AND BROCCOLI

Makes 4 to 6 servings

3 tablespoons vegetable oil

1 pound boneless, skinless chicken breast, cut into 1-inch cubes

1 bunch green onions, sliced

2 tablespoons finely chopped garlic

2 tablespoons minced fresh ginger

1 cup chicken stock or water

3 tablespoons soy sauce

2 tablespoons cider vinegar or rice vinegar

2 tablespoons sugar

2 tablespoons cornstarch

4 cups (1 bunch) broccoli florets

1. Heat the oil in a wok or large sauté pan over medium heat. Add the chicken and cook, stirring the chicken occasionally to cook it evenly on all sides, until it is golden brown, about 5 minutes. Transfer the cooked chicken to a plate and set aside.

2. Add the green onions, garlic, and ginger to the pan and cook, stirring constantly, until fragrant, about 30 seconds.

3. In a medium bowl, combine the chicken stock or water, soy sauce, vinegar, sugar, and cornstarch. Mix with a whisk until there are no clumps and set aside.

4. Add the broccoli to the pan. Add the cornstarch mixture and stir to coat the broccoli.

5. Stir in the chicken, cover the pan with a lid or aluminum foil, and cook on medium-high heat until the broccoli is bright green and cooked through, 3 to 5 minutes.

CHEESEBURGERS

Makes 4 burgers

1½ pounds ground beef

1 teaspoon salt

⅛ teaspoon ground black pepper

2 tablespoons vegetable oil

4 slices American, cheddar, or other cheese (optional)

4 hamburger-style buns

4 tomato slices

4 lettuce leaves

Mustard, to taste

Ketchup, to taste

1. In a large bowl, mix the ground beef with the salt and pepper.

2. Divide the meat into 4 portions (about 6 ounces each). Form each portion into a ball by gently tossing it from one hand to the other and then flatten each portion into a patty. Make the patty as thick or thin as you would like.

3. Heat the oil in a large cast-iron or stainless steel skillet over medium-low heat for 3 to 5 minutes. Add the patties to the hot pan and cook, flipping once, until well browned on each side, about 5 minutes per side. Ground beef needs to be cooked until the juices run clear when you pierce a burger with a knife and the meat reaches an internal temperature of 160°F.

4. If you are using cheese, top the hamburgers during the last 2 minutes of cooking so the cheese can melt.

5. To serve the burgers, place them on the buns and top each one with tomato, lettuce, mustard, and ketchup.

What's in a Fast-Food Hamburger?

Compare the few simple ingredients in a homemade burger (beef, salt, pepper) to what might be in a typical fast-food version:

Beef	Beef fat
Salt	Citric acid
Pepper	Autolyzed yeast extract
Sugar	Turmeric
Onion powder	Calcium silicate
Natural flavor	Garlic powder
Artificial flavor	Dried beef extract
Maltodextrin	Oil
Beef broth	Caramel color
Yeast extract	Tamarind
Lactic acid	Annatto

Think like a Chef

Be adventurous with your burgers! Try topping them with different ingredients to create different flavor profiles. You could also use different buns, like pretzel buns, English muffins, or even your favorite sandwich bread.

Buffalo Chicken Burgers: ground chicken patties + blue cheese + scallions + hot sauce

Fusion Burgers: grilled pineapple + Teriyaki Sauce (page 144)

Tex Mex Burgers: pepper Jack cheese + Guacamole (page 154) + diced tomatoes + cilantro

Crunchy BBQ Burgers: barbeque sauce + Coleslaw (page 76) + Pickle Chips (page 152)

QUICK AND EASY MACARONI AND CHEESE

Makes 6 to 8 servings

1 pound elbow macaroni

4 cups shredded cheddar cheese

5 tablespoons all-purpose flour

1½ teaspoons salt

2¼ cups milk

2 tablespoons unsalted butter

1. Bring a large pot of salted water to a boil over high heat. Add the macaroni and stir gently as the noodles soften in the boiling water to make sure they don't stick together. Cook the macaroni until just barely tender, about 8 minutes. Drain the macaroni in a colander, return to the pot, and set aside.

2. In a medium bowl, combine the cheese, flour, and salt.

3. In a small pot over medium heat, warm the milk until it is hot but not boiling.

4. Return the pot with the macaroni to the stove over medium heat. Add the butter and the cheese mixture to the macaroni, stir until everything is combined, and cook until the cheese just starts to melt, about 1 minute.

5. Add the warm milk to the macaroni and cook, stirring occasionally, until the cheese is melted and the sauce is thickened and creamy, 3 to 5 minutes. Serve immediately.

Think Like a Chef

You can use any kind of cheese you like to make mac and cheese — even blue cheese, goat cheese, or smoked gouda. Just keep the overall amount of cheese the same and use mostly soft varieties that melt very well (although the occasional bit of grated Parmesan for flavor never hurt).

Green Chile Mac and Cheese: Monterey Jack cheese + green chiles + tomatillos + cilantro

Shrimp Mac and Cheese: Havarti cheese + cooked shrimp + smoked paprika + green onions

Tomato-Basil Mac and Cheese: mozzarella + tomato + prosciutto + basil + panko bread crumbs

RAMEN NOODLE STIR FRY

Makes 4 to 6 servings

1 package instant ramen noodles

¼ cup soy sauce

1¾ cups chicken stock

2 tablespoons sugar

2 tablespoons cornstarch

2 teaspoons sesame oil

3 tablespoons vegetable oil

1 tablespoon finely chopped garlic

1 tablespoon minced fresh ginger

1 tablespoon chopped onion

1 pound boneless, skinless chicken breasts or thighs, cut into ½-inch cubes

2 cups broccoli florets

1. Place the ramen noodles in a medium bowl and cover them with hot tap water. Discard the seasoning packet. Once softened, drain the noodles in a colander.

2. Meanwhile, in a small bowl, combine the soy sauce, chicken stock, sugar, cornstarch, and sesame oil. Mix until there are no lumps remaining and set aside.

3. Heat a wok or large sauté pan over medium heat.

4. Combine the vegetable oil, garlic, ginger, and onion in the pan and cook, stirring with a wooden spoon, until softened and fragrant, about 3 minutes.

5. Add the chicken to the pan and cook, stirring, until the chicken begins to brown around the edges, about 3 minutes.

6. Add the cornstarch mixture, noodles, and broccoli.

7. Cover the pan with a lid or aluminum foil and simmer until the broccoli is tender and the chicken is cooked through, 3 to 5 minutes.

Did You Know?

Instant ramen noodles are an inexpensive, convenient, and versatile food that is eaten in China and Japan. To make them, flour, water, and other ingredients are kneaded together into a dough and then cut into fine strands. Then the noodles are pre-steamed and shaped to fit into square or circular packaging before being fried in oil, dried, and packaged. Since they've been precooked, they only need to be softened briefly in hot water or boiled gently for several minutes before using.

Peeling Ginger

One of the best ways to remove the skin from ginger is with a teaspoon. Scrape across the skin of the ginger with a teaspoon; the skin will be the only thing removed, preventing any waste of usable ginger and leaving the whole root for you to use in your delicious creation. Slice, chop, or grate according to how you plan to use it.

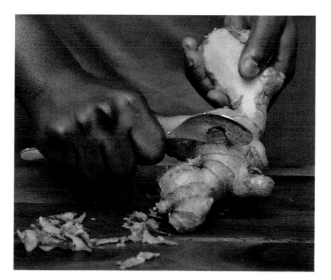

BEEF OR CHICKEN SATAY WITH PEANUT SAUCE

Makes about 12 skewers (6 servings)

Satay Skewers

½ cup soy sauce

1 tablespoon vegetable oil

1 tablespoon lemon juice

1 tablespoon chopped ginger

1 tablespoon chopped garlic

1 tablespoon honey

1½ teaspoons curry powder

1½ pounds beef or boneless chicken thighs or breast

12 bamboo skewers (soaked in water for 20 minutes)

Sauce

½ cup coconut milk

¼ cup peanut butter

¼ cup water

2 tablespoons lime juice

½ teaspoon sugar

1. To make the satay skewers, in a small bowl, mix together the soy sauce, oil, lemon juice, ginger, garlic, honey, and curry powder to make a marinade.

2. Cut the beef or chicken into strips about the width of one or two fingers, and place them in a bowl or zip-top bag. Add the marinade and refrigerate the meat, covered or sealed, for 1 to 8 hours.

3. Remove the beef or chicken from the marinade. Save the marinade to use in the sauce.

4. Put the meat on the skewers by pushing the skewer through the bottom, center, and top of each piece of meat.

5. To make the sauce, in a medium pot, combine the reserved marinade with the coconut milk, peanut butter, water, lime juice, and sugar. Cook on low heat, stirring occasionally, until the sauce comes to a simmer, about 3 minutes. Set the sauce aside.

6. Preheat an outdoor grill to medium-high heat. Make sure that the grill bars are clean and hot, to keep the meat from sticking to the grill.

7. Reduce the grill temperature to medium and grill the beef or chicken until it has grill marks and it is fully cooked, about 6 minutes. (Or, if you are using a charcoal grill, move the meat to a cooler part of the grill to cook.)

8. Serve with the warm peanut sauce.

Chef's Note

Soaking the skewers before grilling keeps the wood or bamboo from burning over the hot heat.

Safety First

Remember, have an adult light the grill.

Did You Know?

Satay, originally spelled "Sate," is a dish that originated on Indonesia's island of Java. It consists of a skewered meat like chicken, shrimp, pork, or lamb (or tofu can also be used) that is marinated, grilled, and usually served with a spicy dipping sauce of some type, like the peanut sauce in this recipe. Other international variations include the Japanese yakitori, the Turkish shish kebab, and shashlik from the Middle East. All are common street foods that are eaten for breakfast, lunch, and dinner.

Serving Suggestion

If you'd like, serve these skewers with Coconut Rice (page 135).

BBQ GRILLED CHICKEN

Makes 4 servings

4 pieces boneless skinless chicken breast

2 tablespoons Spice Rub for Meat
(recipe follows)

2 teaspoons vegetable oil

½ cup Texas-Style BBQ Sauce (page 145),
or your favorite store-bought variety

1. In a medium bowl or zip-top plastic bag, combine
   the chicken with the spice rub and oil and rub
   the spice mixture into the chicken until it is
   coated. Let the chicken marinate for at least
   15 minutes.

2. Heat a clean grill to medium-high heat and
   grill the chicken for about 5 minutes. Turn the
   chicken over and reduce the grill temperature to
   low. (Or, if you are using a charcoal grill, move
   the chicken to a cooler part of the grill.) Cook for
   another 10 minutes.

3. Brush the barbeque sauce over the chicken
   and continue to cook until the juices run clear
   when you pierce it with a knife and the chicken
   reaches an internal temperature of 165°F, 5 to
   8 minutes.

Safety First

Remember, have an adult light the grill.

SPICE RUB FOR MEAT

Makes ½ cup

3 tablespoons chili powder

1 tablespoon cumin

1½ teaspoons paprika

1½ teaspoons salt

1 teaspoon garlic powder

1 teaspoon sugar

1 teaspoon all-purpose flour

½ teaspoon onion powder

½ teaspoon dried oregano

¼ teaspoon ground black pepper

Combine all of the ingredients together in
a bowl or airtight container and whisk to
incorporate. Store in an airtight container at room
temperature.

SIMPLE SIDES AND SAUCES

Pan-Steamed Carrots, Broccoli, Cauliflower, or Green Beans

Sautéed Zucchini or Yellow Squash

Grilled Mixed Vegetables

Roasted or Baked Potatoes or Sweet Potatoes

Buttered Broccoli

Grandma's Smashed Potatoes

Mashed Sweet Potatoes

Oven-Baked Sweet Potato Fries

Refried Beans

Stewed Red Beans

Braised Collard Greens

Baked Southern Cheese Grits

Coconut Rice

Double-Stuffed Potatoes

Oven-Roasted Potatoes

Naan-Style Flatbread

Grandma's Tomato Sauce

Warm Cheesy Sauce

Pesto Sauce

Teriyaki Sauce

Texas-Style BBQ Sauce

BASIC VEGETABLE COOKERY

Simply prepared vegetables make a great side dish with almost any kind of meal. You don't even need a recipe to make them, just follow these basic techniques. You can dress them up with grated cheese, your favorite sauce, or even just a little butter. They are also good with dips and salad dressings, or they can be the starting point to create your own recipes.

Preparing Vegetables

Vegetables (and fruits) should be rinsed under cold running water to remove all traces of dirt and contaminants. You can either trim and cut up vegetables before cooking or cook them whole.

When Is It Done?

Cook vegetables until they can easily be cut with a fork; chefs call this **"fork tender."** They should also be bright in color.

Boiled Vegetables

Boiling is an easy cooking technique that works for most vegetables. The vegetables should be the same size and shape to make sure they cook evenly. Choose a pot that is big enough to hold all the water and vegetables comfortably, and have a colander or strainer ready to drain the vegetables once they are cooked. Soft vegetables, such as broccoli or green beans, will cook faster than hard vegetables, such as potatoes or beets.

To boil vegetables: Wash the vegetables and peel or cut them into pieces, if desired. Fill a large pot with enough water that the vegetables will be fully immersed once added. Add salt to the water (about 1 teaspoon is usually a good amount). Bring the water to a rolling boil and add the vegetables carefully so that the water does not splash up at you. Cook the vegetables until fork tender. Drain in a colander.

Chef's Notes

Starchy root vegetables such as potatoes should be started in cold water and then brought to a boil in order to cook evenly.

Leave the lid *off* of green vegetables such as green beans and broccoli, or they will turn an unappetizing dark green color.

Leave the lid *on* red and white vegetables such as red cabbage, beets, and turnips; this will help to retain their colors after cooking.

Shocking

Shocking is a technique that chefs use when precooking vegetables. Once the vegetables have been boiled, remove them from the pot and plunge them into a bowl of water and ice. This stops the cooking and, for green vegetables, brings out a color pigment called chlorophyll so that the vegetables stay nice and green. The precooked vegetables can then be reheated in a sauté pan using butter or a small amount of water, or they can be incorporated into other recipes.

Steamed Vegetables

Any vegetable that can be boiled can also be steamed. Since the vegetables aren't submerged in liquid, steamed vegetables may be less soggy than boiled and often have better nutritional value. Vegetables can be steamed using a metal steaming insert or an Asian bamboo steamer (see page 31).

To steam vegetables: Wash the vegetables and peel or cut them into pieces if desired. Place a steaming insert into a pot and pour 1 to 2 inches of water into the pot. Bring the water to a boil, place the vegetables in the basket, and cover the pot with a lid. Steam the vegetables until tender, 3 to 6 minutes depending on the amount, type, and density of the vegetables. Season the steamed vegetables however you'd like—for example, with salt, pepper, fresh herbs, or butter.

Grilled Vegetables

High-moisture or tender vegetables can be grilled raw, but dense or starchy vegetables should be boiled first—called **par-boiling** (short for "partially boiling")—before grilling to make sure they cook all the way through. These par-boiled vegetables should not be fork tender, but still firm and crunchy. Some examples of vegetables that can be grilled from a raw state are eggplant, onions, zucchini, peppers, tomatoes, and mushrooms. Vegetables that are typically par-boiled include potatoes, carrots, and beets. The grill should be set on medium or medium-high heat and cleaned very well with a grill brush before grilling in order to keep the vegetables from sticking.

Vegetables can also be marinated (see page 32) before grilling, using a variety of ingredients such as salad dressings, mustard, ketchup, soy sauce, or even barbeque sauce.

To grill vegetables: Preheat the grill to medium or medium-high and clean it with a wire grill brush. Wash the vegetables and peel or cut them into pieces, if desired. Season or marinate the vegetables if you'd like. Grill the vegetables for several minutes per side, or until they are tender and have distinctive grill marks.

Roasted Vegetables

Thick-skinned whole vegetables such as potatoes, carrots, winter squash, peppers, eggplant, and even mushrooms are great for roasting. The skin protects the interior from drying or scorching. Roasting is also excellent for halved, cut, sliced, or diced vegetables. Toss the vegetables with oil before roasting to keep them from drying out and to help them cook evenly. Add seasonings such as salt, pepper, spice blends, or garlic prior to cooking and then finish the cooked vegetables with butter or fresh herbs right before serving. You could also marinate the vegetables before roasting.

To roast vegetables: Preheat the oven to 350°F. Wash and scrub the vegetables, and cut them into pieces if you'd like. Toss them with vegetable oil or olive oil (or a marinade), season with salt and pepper or other seasonings, and then spread the vegetables on a baking sheet or in a casserole dish. Roast until a fork can be inserted easily into the center.

Roasting Broccoli and Cauliflower

Broccoli and cauliflower makes a wonderful roasted vegetables and can be roasted relatively quickly. They are also easy to cut up so they can be prepared in almost no time at all.

Sautéed or Stir-Fried Vegetables

Tender vegetables such as zucchini, yellow squash, mushrooms, spinach, peppers, and onions are good for sautéing or stir frying. Select a cooking fat, such as olive oil, peanut oil, or butter, that you think will taste good with the vegetables. Oils such as olive, peanut, or vegetable are best for cooking over high heat. Butter can be used as long as the temperature is kept low to avoid burning it.

To sauté or stir fry vegetables: Wash the vegetables, peel if desired, and cut them into pieces. Heat the oil or butter in a sauté pan or wok over high heat. Add the vegetables and cook, stirring constantly with a wooden spoon or tongs to keep them from sticking to the pan and to ensure even cooking. Make sure that the pan is not too crowded (you may need to cook in batches if you're making a large amount). Cook until the vegetables are fork tender, add any seasonings you'd like, and serve immediately.

PAN-STEAMED CARROTS, BROCCOLI, CAULIFLOWER, OR GREEN BEANS

Makes 5 to 6 servings

1 pound carrots, broccoli, cauliflower, or green beans

2 tablespoons unsalted butter

2 teaspoons chopped fresh parsley

Salt and pepper, to taste

1. Wash the vegetables and peel, trim, and cut them into slices or small pieces as needed.

2. Add about 1 inch of water to a large sauté pan and bring to a boil.

3. Add the vegetables and cover the pan with a lid.

4. Pan steam the vegetables until they are fully cooked and tender to the bite, 5 to 6 minutes.

5. Drain the excess water from the pan. Return the pan to the heat; add the butter, parsley, and salt and pepper. Serve immediately.

Kitchen Vocabulary

Foods that are seasoned **"to taste"** are literally tasted as the seasoning is added to see when enough has been added.

SAUTÉED ZUCCHINI OR YELLOW SQUASH

Makes 5 to 6 servings

½ pound (2 or 3) zucchini or yellow squash

2 teaspoons vegetable oil

1 tablespoon unsalted butter

½ teaspoon garlic powder

½ teaspoon onion powder

Salt and pepper, to taste

1. Wash and cut the ends off of the zucchini or yellow squash. Slice into ¼-inch-thick rounds.

2. Heat a large sauté pan over medium heat and add the oil and butter.

3. Add the squash and cook, stirring or tossing from time to time, until the vegetables are fully cooked, about 5 minutes.

4. Add the garlic powder, onion powder, and salt and pepper and stir to combine. Serve immediately.

GRILLED MIXED VEGETABLES

Makes 5 to 6 servings

1 pound assorted vegetables, such as eggplant, tomatoes, zucchini, mushrooms, onions, or bell peppers

Marinade

2 tablespoons vegetable oil

1 teaspoon soy sauce

1 teaspoon lemon juice

1 teaspoon garlic powder

1. Wash the vegetables, if needed, and cut them into slices about ½ inch thick and place in a medium bowl.

2. To make the marinade, combine the oil, soy sauce, lemon juice, and garlic powder. Pour the marinade over the vegetables, coating them evenly.

3. Heat the grill to medium-high heat.

4. Place the vegetables on the grill and cook for several minutes per side, until they are tender. Serve immediately.

ROASTED OR BAKED POTATOES OR SWEET POTATOES

Makes 6 servings

6 baking potatoes or sweet potatoes

Preheat the oven to 425°F. Scrub the potatoes and blot dry. Pierce the potatoes with a knife or kitchen fork. Bake until tender and cooked through, about 1 hour.

Chef's Notes

To serve, pinch or cut open the potato and top with cheese, butter, sour cream, or bacon bits.

Piercing the potatoes before baking allows the steam that develops from moisture in the potato to escape without the potato exploding during baking.

BUTTERED BROCCOLI

Makes about 5 servings

4 cups broccoli florets

2 tablespoons unsalted butter

½ teaspoon salt

Pinch of ground black pepper

1. Bring a medium pot of water to a boil over high heat.

2. Add the broccoli and cook until it is tender and bright green, about 4 minutes.

3. Drain the broccoli and transfer to a bowl. Add the butter, salt, and pepper and toss together.

Chef's Note

This method and recipe can be used for many vegetables, such as carrots and Brussels sprouts. The cooking time will depend on the vegetable, so start checking for doneness while the vegetables are still bright in color.

Kitchen Vocabulary

Tender in cooking terms means to cook until there is no "crunch" when you bite into a food. Chefs call this "tender to the bite!"

What Is Hoisin Sauce?

A sweet, spicy, dark red sauce made from soybeans, vinegar, sugar, garlic, and various spices, hoisin sauce is widely used in southern Chinese cooking.

Think like a Chef

It's easy to love vegetables when you add your favorite seasonings or sauce!

Italian-Style Broccoli: garlic + chili flakes + seasoned bread crumbs + Parmesan cheese

Asian-Style Broccoli: sesame oil + hoisin sauce + sesame seeds + slivered almonds

GRANDMA'S SMASHED POTATOES

Makes 6 servings

2 pounds russet potatoes, peeled and cut into quarters
1 cup milk
4 tablespoons (½ stick) butter
1½ teaspoons salt
Pinch of ground black pepper

1. Place the potatoes in a medium pot and cover with cold water.

2. Bring the water to a boil over high heat and then boil the potatoes until tender, about 20 minutes.

3. Drain the potatoes in a colander and set aside.

4. In the same pot, heat the milk to a simmer over medium heat, then add the butter, salt, and pepper.

5. When the butter has melted, add the potatoes to the milk mixture and smash with a potato masher. Serve immediately.

Chef's Note

A potato masher is a handled tool with a wire end that mashes cooked potatoes. If you don't have a potato masher, you can use a ricer or food mill to make mashed potatoes.

Did You Know?

Each American eats over 100 pounds of potatoes a year, according to the National Potato Council. Potatoes are the leading vegetable crop in the United States, with over half the crop processed into French fries, and much of the rest sold as fresh potatoes and chips.

Which Potatoes?

Most potatoes can be classified into one of two varieties. High-starch potatoes, such as russet and Idaho, have thick skins, tend to be white, and are good for sautéing, grilling, baking, and frying (what are known as "dry heat" methods).

High-moisture potatoes are small to medium in size, have thin skins, and tend to be yellow or red. They are best used for moist cooking methods such as boiling, steaming, and making soups and stews since their moisture keeps the potatoes from falling apart when cooked in liquid.

Think Like a Chef

Who doesn't love potatoes? And they go with almost anything — like sautéed onions or any type of cheese. Just make sure to add a bit at a time to get the best flavor and consistency. And don't over mix your potatoes, or they can become gummy.

Loaded Mashed Potatoes: cheddar cheese + bacon + scallions

Mashed Potatoes Provençal: Niçoise olives + rosemary + thyme

MASHED SWEET POTATOES

Makes 4 servings

4 sweet potatoes

4 tablespoons (½ stick) butter

1½ teaspoons sugar

1 teaspoon salt

Pinch of ground black pepper

1. Peel the sweet potatoes and cut each one into 8 pieces.

2. Place the sweet potatoes in a large pot and cover with cold water. Bring to a boil over medium heat. Boil the sweet potatoes until they are fork tender (see page 124), 30 to 35 minutes.

3. Drain the potatoes and transfer them back to the pot or to a large bowl.

4. Add the butter, sugar, salt, and pepper.

5. Mash the potatoes with a stiff whisk, a masher, an electric beater, or a stand mixer fitted with a paddle attachment until they are smooth. Serve immediately.

Chef's Note

These sweet potatoes can also be eaten un-mashed. Serve the potatoes after adding the seasoning ingredients in Step 4.

Did You Know?

Sweet potatoes are versatile Native American plants that are extremely nutritious: They contain high amounts of vitamins A and C as well as potassium, calcium, and fiber. Soft and creamy, they can be eaten savory, as in this mashed potato recipe, or sweet, in pies and desserts. While orange is the most common color, they also come in purple, white, yellow, and even pink.

OVEN-BAKED SWEET POTATO FRIES

Makes 4 to 6 servings

4 sweet potatoes

2 tablespoons vegetable oil

1 teaspoon salt

Pinch of ground black pepper

1. Preheat the oven to 400°F. Line a baking sheet with aluminum foil.

2. Peel the sweet potatoes and cut them lengthwise into 6 or 8 long wedges, depending on the size of the sweet potato.

3. In a large bowl, combine the sweet potatoes, oil, salt, and pepper. Toss until the sweet potatoes are well coated.

4. Evenly space the sweet potatoes in one layer on the prepared baking sheet. Bake for 35 to 40 minutes, until light brown and crispy.

REFRIED BEANS

Makes 6 to 8 servings

2 tablespoons oil

1 cup chopped onions

1 tablespoon finely chopped garlic

Two 15-ounce cans pinto beans, drained

1 cup chopped tomato

½ cup water

¼ cup Texas-Style BBQ Sauce (page 145), or your favorite store-bought variety

1 teaspoon dried oregano

1 teaspoon salt

½ teaspoon ground cumin

¼ teaspoon ground black pepper

1. Heat the oil in a heavy pot over medium heat. Add the onions and cook, stirring with a wooden spoon, until lightly browned, about 6 minutes. Add the garlic and cook, stirring, until fragrant and softened, about 2 minutes.

2. Add the beans, tomato, water, barbeque sauce, oregano, salt, cumin, and pepper.

3. Reduce the heat to low and cook until the beans are soft and the mixture has thickened, about 30 minutes.

4. Remove from the heat and puree the mixture with a hand blender or potato masher before serving.

STEWED RED BEANS

Makes about 2 cups (about 3 servings)

1 teaspoon olive oil

1 cup chopped onions

1 red, yellow, or green bell pepper, chopped

One 15-ounce can red beans, drained

½ cup chopped tomato

¼ cup water

3 cloves garlic, finely chopped

½ teaspoon oregano

½ teaspoon ground cumin

½ teaspoon salt

¼ teaspoon ground black pepper

1. Heat the oil in a medium saucepan over medium heat. Add the onions and peppers and cook, stirring occasionally, until the onions soften and begin to brown, 5 to 8 minutes.

2. Add the beans, tomato, water, garlic, oregano, cumin, salt, and pepper.

3. Cook, stirring with a wooden spoon, until the beans begin to soften and the mixture thickens, about 15 minutes.

4. Remove from the heat and serve.

BRAISED COLLARD GREENS

Makes 6 servings

2 pounds collard greens or kale

2 ounces (about 6 strips) bacon, diced

½ cup diced onions

2 cloves garlic, minced

½ ham hock (optional)

1 cup chicken or vegetable stock

Salt, to taste

Ground black pepper, to taste

1. Preheat the oven to 350°F.

2. Remove the stems from the greens and discard, and wash the greens thoroughly.

3. Bring a large pot of salted water to a boil over high heat. Add the greens and blanch for about 1 minute, then drain. Chop the blanched greens and set them aside.

4. In a large ovenproof skillet, cook the bacon over medium heat until it is crispy and the fat has been rendered. Add the onions and cook, stirring frequently, until translucent, about 3 minutes. Add the garlic and cook until aromatic, about 1 minute.

5. Add the ham hock, if using, along with the blanched greens and the stock, and season with salt and pepper.

6. Transfer the pan to the preheated oven and cook for 30 to 45 minutes, until the greens are tender.

7. Use a slotted spoon to transfer the greens from the pan to a bowl. Transfer the skillet with the remaining liquid to the stove and cook over medium-high heat until it is slightly thickened, about 5 minutes. Add the liquid back to the greens and add more salt and pepper to taste, if necessary.

Chef's Note

A ham hock is a part of a pig's leg. When you add it to the greens, it gives them a nice meaty flavor.

Kitchen Vocabulary

When fat is **rendered,** that means it melts away from the piece of meat that's cooking and becomes liquid in the pan.

BAKED SOUTHERN CHEESE GRITS

Makes 6 servings

4 tablespoons (½ stick) butter

1 tablespoon minced garlic

1 tablespoon minced onion

2 cups water

2 cups milk

Salt, to taste

1 cup yellow stone-ground grits

6 ounces cream cheese, softened

2½ cups grated cheddar cheese

3 tablespoons snipped chives

Ground black pepper, to taste

1. Preheat the oven to 350°F.

2. Heat 2 tablespoons of the butter in a large saucepan over medium heat. Add the garlic and onion and cook, stirring with a wooden spoon, until softened, about 2 minutes. Add the water and milk, season with salt, and bring to a boil. Reduce the heat to a simmer.

3. Gradually add the grits in a thin stream, whisking constantly to prevent lumps from forming. Cook the grits for about 15 minutes, stirring frequently to dissolve any lumps.

4. Remove the pan from the heat and stir in the cream cheese, ½ cup of the cheddar cheese, and 2 tablespoons of the chives. Season with salt and pepper. Use the remaining 2 tablespoons butter to grease a baking dish, then add the grits to the baking dish.

5. Bake for about 1 hour. Top with the remaining 2 cups cheddar cheese, and then continue to bake until the cheese has melted, just a few more minutes.

6. Serve while still hot, garnished with the remaining tablespoon of chives.

COCONUT RICE

Makes 10 servings

1 tablespoon vegetable oil
2 cups long-grain white rice
4 cups water
One 13-ounce can unsweetened coconut milk
½ teaspoon salt
¼ teaspoon ground black pepper

1. Preheat the oven to 350°F.

2. Heat the oil in a medium ovenproof saucepan over medium heat. Add the rice and cook, stirring, until it is coated with oil and heated through, about 1 minute.

3. Add the water, coconut milk, salt, and pepper. Place the lid on the pan and bring to a simmer over medium heat.

4. Transfer the pan, with the lid on, to the oven and cook until the rice is tender, 12 to 15 minutes.

5. Remove the pan from the oven and allow the rice to rest, covered, for 5 minutes. Use a fork to gently stir the rice and separate the grains before serving.

What Is Long-Grain Rice?

There are lots of different kinds of rice, and some of them have longer or shorter grains (see page 99). Short-grain varieties require less cooking liquid and have the most starch. Long-grain rice needs more liquid to cook and has less starch. Brown rice contains the outer coating, called the bran, and takes up to twice as long to cook, regardless of its size.

DOUBLE-STUFFED POTATOES

Makes 8 half potatoes

4 baking potatoes, washed
¾ cup shredded cheddar cheese
¼ cup milk
2 tablespoons sour cream
1 teaspoon salt
½ teaspoon garlic powder
⅛ teaspoon ground black pepper

1. Preheat the oven to 375°F.

2. Place the potatoes on a baking sheet and bake for 45 minutes to 1 hour (depending on the size), until a toothpick can be easily inserted into the center. Remove the potatoes from the oven and let cool.

3. Once cooled, cut the potatoes in half lengthwise and use a spoon to scoop out the centers into a mixing bowl. Set the empty potato skins aside to use later.

4. Add the cheese, milk, sour cream, salt, garlic powder, and pepper to the potatoes in the bowl, and use a potato masher to fully combine all the ingredients.

5. Divide the mashed potato mixture evenly among the reserved potato skins. Return the potatoes to the baking sheet and bake for about 20 minutes, until the potatoes begin to brown on the top and are very hot.

Chef's Note

You could add many different ingredients to the mashed potato mixture, such as chopped bacon, cooked chicken, chives, green onions, or ham.

OVEN-ROASTED POTATOES

Makes 4 to 6 servings

2 pounds potatoes, any variety

2 tablespoons extra-virgin olive oil

½ cup chicken or vegetable stock

1 teaspoon salt

⅛ teaspoon ground black pepper

1. Preheat the oven to 375°F.

2. You may peel the potatoes, or leave the skin on. Cut the potatoes in half lengthwise.

3. Lay the potatoes flat on a cutting board and carefully slice them into ¼-inch pieces.

4. Pour the oil into a baking dish large enough to hold the potatoes spread into one layer. Arrange the potatoes in the pan and add the stock.

5. Season with the salt and pepper.

6. Bake until the potatoes are golden brown, 35 to 45 minutes.

Think like a Chef

Toss the chopped potatoes with different ingredients before or after you roast them to come up with new variations.

Spiced Roasted Potatoes: chili powder + turmeric + ground cumin + green onions

Tangy Roasted Potatoes: malt vinegar + sea salt + chives

Pesto Roasted Tomatoes: Pesto Sauce (page 143) + cherry tomatoes + lemon juice

Variation

FANNED POTATOES

To cut the potatoes into fan shapes, first slice each peeled potato in half lengthwise. Place the flat side of the potato on the cutting board. Cut the potato into thin slices, but make sure to leave the slices attached at the back of the potato. Sprinkle with salt.

Place the cut potatoes in the baking dish. Replace the olive oil and vegetable stock from the recipe with butter and water. Bake at 375°F until the potatoes are golden brown, about 45 minutes. Sprinkle with chopped fresh parsley and serve.

Chef's Notes

Russet potatoes are one kind that are good for roasting. Other types of potatoes are also excellent for roasting, such as Yukon Gold and fingerlings. These varieties have thin skins, so they don't need to be peeled before you cook them.

Certain vegetables, such as potatoes, **oxidize** (turn brown) when peeled or cut and exposed to air. Keep them in a bowl of water until ready to cook to prevent this from happening.

Roasted Potato Salad

Roasting the potatoes offers a way to add another layer of flavor to the common picnic-type potato salad. Use red or russet potatoes for the best result. The amount of starch in these potatoes makes them ideal for making a great potato salad. Throw in some bacon, eggs, green onion, celery, mustard, mayo, or any other ingredients you like. It is easy to make and you can adjust the ingredients to suit your own personal taste.

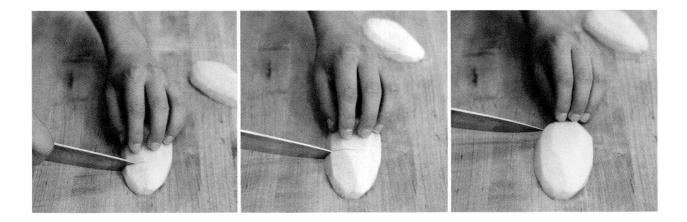

NAAN-STYLE FLATBREAD

Makes 5 flatbreads

1 cup milk

2 tablespoons vegetable oil, plus more for the sauté pan

¼ cup yogurt, sour cream, or ricotta cheese

1 egg

2½ cups all-purpose flour, plus more for dusting

½ cup whole wheat flour

1 tablespoon sugar

1 teaspoon instant dry yeast

1 teaspoon baking powder

1 teaspoon salt

1. In the bowl of a stand mixer fitted with the dough hook attachment, combine the milk, oil, yogurt, egg, all-purpose flour, whole wheat flour, sugar, yeast, and baking powder.

2. Add the salt and mix on low speed until the dough is smooth and elastic, about 5 minutes.

3. Cover the bowl with plastic wrap and let the dough rise in a warm place until doubled in size, about 30 minutes.

4. Dust a clean surface with flour and cut the dough into 5 equal pieces.

5. Roll the dough into balls and set them on the counter to rest, covered with plastic wrap or a clean kitchen towel, for 10 minutes.

6. Using a rolling pin, roll the dough into flat disks, 8 to 10 inches in diameter.

7. Heat about 1 teaspoon of oil in a 10-inch sauté pan over medium heat. Add one of the pieces of dough.

8. Cook the dough over medium heat until the bottom of the bread is golden brown, 2 to 3 minutes. With a pair of tongs or a metal spatula, flip the bread over and cook the other side until golden brown, 2 to 3 minutes more. Remove from the pan and set aside.

9. Repeat with the remaining pieces of dough, adding more oil as needed.

Chef's Note

Naan is a flatbread common in Indian cuisine (as well as in other regions). The bread is often torn and used to scoop up savory dishes. But you can serve naan with other foods, too, such as Hummus (page 153). You could also use it as a base for a pizza or as a sandwich wrap.

GRANDMA'S TOMATO SAUCE

Makes about 2 quarts

2 teaspoons extra-virgin olive oil

1 cup chopped onion

1 tablespoon finely chopped garlic

One 28-ounce can tomato puree

One 28-ounce can whole peeled tomatoes, drained

2 tablespoons chopped fresh basil

1 tablespoon sugar

½ teaspoon salt

¼ teaspoon minced fresh oregano

⅛ teaspoon ground black pepper

1. Heat the oil in a medium saucepan over medium heat. Add the onions and cook, stirring frequently, until the onions are soft, about 5 minutes. Add the garlic and stir to incorporate.

2. Add the tomato puree and tomatoes and stir to incorporate.

3. Reduce the heat to low and cook, uncovered, until the sauce is slightly thickened and flavorful, 30 to 40 minutes.

4. Add the basil, sugar, salt, oregano, and pepper.

5. For a smooth sauce, puree the sauce with a stick blender or in batches in a regular blender. Otherwise, it can be served chunky.

Chef's Note
Once cooled down, this large batch can be refrigerated in an airtight container for up to 5 days or frozen.

WARM CHEESY SAUCE

Makes 2½ cups

1 cup milk

4 teaspoons cornstarch

4 cups (1 pound) shredded cheddar, American, or Monterey Jack cheese

Pinch of ground black pepper

1. In a saucepan, whisk together the milk and cornstarch.

2. Cook over medium heat, stirring occasionally, until the milk begins to boil and thicken, about 5 minutes.

3. Reduce the heat to low and add the cheese and pepper. Stir until the cheese is melted and the sauce is thick. Stirring the cheese in a figure-eight pattern will help keep the sauce from getting stringy and sticking to the bottom of the pan.

4. Serve the sauce immediately, or refrigerate in a covered container until ready to use. If it is chilled, reheat the sauce in a small saucepan over medium heat before using.

Chef's Notes
This sauce is great for topping nachos, broccoli, or pasta. But you could also add it to almost anything you like!

For a thinner consistency, add more milk 1 tablespoon at a time until the sauce is as thin as you would like.

PESTO SAUCE

Makes 1 cup

- 5 cups fresh basil leaves
- ½ cup grated Parmesan cheese
- ¼ cup extra-virgin olive oil
- 2 to 3 cloves garlic, peeled
- 2 tablespoons water
- 1 teaspoon salt

Combine the basil, cheese, oil, garlic, water, and salt in a blender or food processor and pulse on and off until the mixture is smooth. Basil is a very delicate herb, so do not blend the mixture more than necessary, or the sauce will become dark-colored and bitter.

Chef's Notes

Pesto sauce often contains nuts. You can add ¼ cup of pine nuts, walnuts, or almonds to the mixture before it is pureed in the blender.

Storing pesto in the refrigerator with a thin layer of olive oil on top will keep it green and fresh for several days.

Did You Know?

The first pesto is said to have been made in the Liguria region of Northern Italy, known for producing superior quality basil, pine nuts, Parmesan cheese, garlic, salt, and olive oil, the six main ingredients of pesto. It's named after the mortar and pestle—the traditional tools used to pound the ingredients into a paste.

Think like a Chef

The name "pesto" comes from the same Latin root as "pestle," and in its simplest form, pesto is made by crushing a few key ingredients together. So, you can make your own pesto and use different herbs or greens of your choice, as well as different nuts and cheeses, crushed together. Arugula is one alternative to using basil. Bell peppers, sun-dried tomatoes, and ricotta cheese are also used to make types of pesto.

TERIYAKI SAUCE

Makes about 1 cup

¼ cup water

1 tablespoon cornstarch

¼ cup soy sauce

3 tablespoons sugar

2 tablespoons white vinegar

2 teaspoons sesame oil

1 tablespoon finely chopped garlic

1 tablespoon minced fresh ginger

1. In a small saucepan, combine the water and cornstarch, stirring to dissolve the cornstarch.

2. Add the soy sauce, sugar, vinegar, sesame oil, garlic, and ginger. Cook over medium heat, stirring occasionally, until the sauce is thickened, about 5 minutes.

Think Like a Chef

Teriyaki sauce is a sweet, Asian-style sauce that can be used in many ways! You can use it as a dip for chicken, a topping for pizza, or a spread on a burger or sandwich. You can also use the sauce as a marinade for chicken, pork, beef, or vegetables before grilling or roasting. Just remember that since this sauce is sweet, it can burn quickly on a grill, so be careful not to cook the items over a very hot flame.

TEXAS-STYLE BBQ SAUCE

Makes 3 cups

1¾ cups ketchup

½ cup white vinegar

¼ cup water

¼ cup brown sugar

2 tablespoons Worcestershire sauce

2 teaspoons paprika

1 tablespoon chili powder

2 teaspoons dry mustard

1 teaspoon salt

½ teaspoon ground black pepper

1. Combine the ketchup, vinegar, water, brown sugar, Worcestershire sauce, paprika, chili powder, mustard, salt, and pepper in a saucepan and whisk until thoroughly blended.

2. Simmer the sauce over low heat until slightly thickened, about 15 minutes.

3. Use immediately, or let cool and then refrigerate in a covered container until ready to use.

Other Styles of Barbeque Sauce

East Carolina Sauce: The simplest and the earliest, popularized by African slaves who also advanced the development of American barbeque. Made with vinegar, ground black pepper, and hot chili pepper flakes, it is used as a "mopping" sauce to baste the meat while it's cooking and as a dipping sauce when the meat is served.

Lexington Dip (a.k.a. Western Carolina Dip or Piedmont Dip): East Carolina Sauce with tomato paste, tomato sauce, or ketchup added.

Kansas City: Thick, reddish-brown, and tomato- or ketchup-based with added sugars, vinegar, and spices, it is usually thick and sweet.

Memphis: Similar to Kansas City style, it typically has the same ingredients, but tends to have a larger percentage of vinegar and use molasses as a sweetener instead of sugar.

Texas: In some older, more traditional restaurants, the sauces are heavily seasoned with cumin, chili peppers, bell peppers or ancho powder, lots of black pepper, fresh onion, and a very small amount of tomato, with little or no sugar, and they often contain meat drippings and smoke flavor because meats are dipped into them. They are medium-thick and often resemble a thin tomato soup.

South Carolina Mustard Sauce: South Carolina is known for its yellow barbeque sauces made primarily of yellow mustard, vinegar, sugar, and spices.

Alabama White Sauce: North Alabama is known for its distinctive white, mayonnaise-based sauce, used on chicken and pork. It is composed of mayonnaise, vinegar, sugar, salt, and black pepper.

SAVORY SNACKS

Sweet and Salty Popcorn

Spiced Mixed Nuts

Soft Pretzels

Pickle Chips

Hummus

Warm Spinach Dip

Guacamole

Tomato Salsa

Green Tomatillo Salsa (Salsa Verde)

Vegetable Summer Rolls with Peanut Dipping Sauce

SWEET AND SALTY POPCORN

Makes about 12 cups

| 2 tablespoons vegetable oil |
| ½ cup popping corn |
| 2 tablespoons sugar |
| 2 teaspoons salt |

1. Heat the oil in a large heavy pot over medium-high heat. Add several kernels of corn and cover the pot.

2. As soon as the kernels pop, carefully add the remaining corn and cover the pot.

3. Using pot holders, carefully shake the pot as the corn begins to pop. Shake the pot occasionally to prevent the popcorn from burning.

4. Once the popping becomes less frequent, turn off the heat.

5. Once the corn has stopped popping, carefully remove the lid and stir in the sugar and salt.

6. Transfer to a bowl and serve immediately.

Think Like a Chef

Make your own gourmet popcorn by tossing the popped kernels with other fun ingredients.

Buffalo Popcorn: butter + hot sauce

Sticky Pecan Popcorn: maple syrup + cinnamon + chopped pecans

Rosemary Popcorn: olive oil + Parmesan cheese + chopped fresh rosemary

Chocolate Coconut Popcorn: coconut oil + coconut flakes + chocolate chunks

SPICED MIXED NUTS

Makes 1 pound

3 tablespoons butter
½ teaspoon Worcestershire sauce
1 pound unsalted mixed nuts (see Chef's Note)
½ teaspoon celery seed
½ teaspoon garlic powder
½ teaspoon chili powder
½ teaspoon salt
¼ teaspoon ground cumin
Pinch of cayenne

1. Preheat the oven to 375°F.

2. In a medium saucepan over medium heat, melt the butter. Add the Worcestershire sauce and cook just until the butter begins to bubble. Add the nuts and stir to coat evenly.

3. Sprinkle the celery seed, garlic powder, chili powder, salt, cumin, and cayenne over the nuts and stir to coat the nuts.

4. Transfer the nuts to a nonstick or well-greased baking sheet and bake, stirring occasionally, until evenly browned, 10 to 12 minutes. Transfer from the baking sheet to a plate and let cool completely before serving.

5. Store in an airtight container for up to 2 weeks.

Think Like a Chef

Sugar and spice and everything nice make for delicious nutty snacks! Substitute these different nuts and spices for the ones used at left.

Cocoa Almonds: almonds + cocoa powder + cinnamon + sugar + sea salt

Curry Cashews: cashews + curry powder

Spicy Chili Peanuts: peanuts + chili powder + cayenne + lime juice

Chef's Note

Premixed packages of nuts can be purchased at the grocery store and usually include peanuts, cashews, almonds, and walnuts. This recipe can be made with any assortment of nuts, or even just one type of nut.

SOFT PRETZELS

Makes 4 pretzels

Dough

2 cups bread flour

1½ teaspoons instant yeast

¾ cup water

½ tablespoon unsalted butter

1 teaspoon honey

2¼ teaspoons salt

Dipping Solution

4 cups water

3 tablespoons baking soda

Coarse sea salt, as needed for sprinkling

1. To make the dough, in a small bowl, mix together the flour and yeast.

2. In the bowl of a stand mixer fitted with the dough hook attachment, combine the water, butter, honey, and salt. Add the flour mixture and mix on low speed until the ingredients are combined, about 1 minute. Raise the speed to medium and mix until the dough is smooth, about 3 minutes.

3. Cover the bowl with plastic wrap and let the dough rise in a warm place until doubled in size, about 20 minutes.

4. Remove the dough from the bowl and divide into 4 equal pieces. Use both hands to roll each piece of dough against the counter into a short log. Place the logs on the counter, loosely cover all of the pieces with plastic wrap, and let rest for 15 minutes.

5. Roll each piece of dough under your palms until it is 30 inches long and tapered so that the center is slightly thicker than the ends.

6. Hold the two ends of the dough in your hands and cross them over each other, to form an X, with the thicker center of the dough at the bottom. Twist the ends again and then bring the two ends down and press each end into the bottom of the pretzel, leaving about 2 inches in between. Press gently to seal the dough.

7. Transfer the pretzels to a parchment-paper-lined baking sheet and cover with plastic wrap. Let the dough rest at room temperature until the pretzels have doubled in size, about 30 minutes. Meanwhile, preheat the oven to 400°F.

8. Place the baking sheet in the refrigerator until the dough forms a skin, about 10 minutes.

9. To make the dipping solution, while the dough is in the refrigerator, combine the water and baking soda in a large bowl. Stir until the baking soda is dissolved.

10. Dip each pretzel in the dipping solution and return to the baking sheet. Sprinkle the pretzels with the salt while they are still wet.

11. Bake the pretzels until they are dark golden brown, 12 to 15 minutes. Transfer them to a wire rack to cool before serving.

Kitchen Science

Yeast is a living organism that needs warmth, moisture, and food to begin fermenting. **Fermentation** is the process of converting sugars into carbon dioxide. The carbon dioxide gas gets trapped in the flour's protein structure, which is formed during mixing. Yeast is sensitive to temperature and will die at 138°F. The ideal temperature for fermentation is between 80°F and 90°F. Lower temperatures will slow down yeast development, and bread dough can be frozen, thawed, and baked without harming the yeast.

PICKLE CHIPS

Makes about 2 quarts

1 pound cucumbers (see Chef's Note)

1 cup water

½ cup white vinegar

¼ cup cider vinegar

6 tablespoons sugar

½ teaspoon mustard seed (any type)

½ teaspoon ground turmeric

½ teaspoon salt

¼ teaspoon celery seed

⅛ teaspoon ground allspice

1. Wash the cucumbers and carefully cut them into ¼-inch-thick slices.

2. In a large pot, combine the water, white vinegar, cider vinegar, sugar, mustard seed, turmeric, salt, celery seed, and allspice. Bring this mixture to a boil over high heat.

3. Add the sliced cucumbers to the boiling liquid and simmer until the cucumbers just begin to soften, about 1 minute.

4. Remove the pot from the heat and let the cucumbers cool for about 20 minutes, stirring occasionally.

5. Transfer the pickles with the cooking liquid to a covered container and refrigerate for at least 2 hours. Serve well chilled.

Chef's Note

This recipe is best when made using Kirby cucumbers, though any cucumber will work. Kirby cucumbers are small cucumbers with tender skin, fewer seeds, and a slightly sweeter flavor than large slicing cucumbers.

Think Like a Chef

You can use this same recipe, substituting some of the ingredients, to make lots of other types of pickles.

Pickled Carrots: baby carrots + garlic + curry paste

Pickled Red Onions: red onion + apple cider vinegar

Pickled Mixed Vegetables: cauliflower + celery + bell pepper

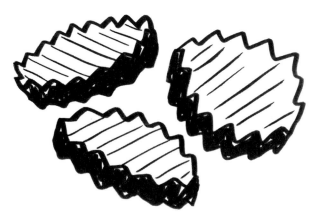

HUMMUS

Makes about 2½ cups

Two 15-ounce cans (about 2½ cups) chickpeas, drained and rinsed

2 to 3 tablespoons tahini (see Chef's Note)

2 tablespoons lemon juice

2 teaspoons salt

1 teaspoon garlic powder

¼ cup water

2 tablespoons olive oil

1. In a food processor fitted with the blade attachment, combine the chickpeas, tahini, lemon juice, salt, and garlic powder.

2. Turn on the food processor and puree until the chickpeas begin to break apart and the ingredients are combined, about 30 seconds.

3. Add the water and oil and puree until smooth, about 1 minute.

Chef's Note
Tahini is the name of pureed sesame seed paste, which is available in most grocery stores. It is sold in cans or jars.

WARM SPINACH DIP

Makes about 3 cups (8 to 10 servings)

- 2 cups cooked chopped spinach (or thawed if frozen), squeezed dry and drained
- 1 cup finely chopped artichoke hearts
- 1 cup sour cream
- ⅓ cup grated Parmesan cheese
- 2 teaspoons minced garlic
- 1 cup grated Monterey Jack cheese
- ¼ teaspoon salt
- ¼ teaspoon ground black pepper

1. Preheat the oven to 350°F.

2. In an ovenproof bowl, stir together the spinach, artichokes, sour cream, Parmesan, and garlic. Add the Monterey Jack cheese, salt, and pepper and stir to combine.

3. Transfer the bowl to the oven and bake until the mixture is very hot and bubbly, 10 to 15 minutes.

4. Carefully remove from the oven and serve hot.

Chef's Note

Have you ever noticed how much spinach shrinks when it's cooked? That's because spinach leaves contain a lot of water, which runs out of the spinach as it cooks, causing the leaves to shrink. Some of that water evaporates, but it is important to drain the rest from the spinach before using, or else your dip will be runny and wet. Press the cooked spinach into a mesh strainer to help squeeze out the extra water.

Serving Suggestion

This dip could also be served in a small, round pumpernickel, rye, or sourdough loaf as a "bowl." To prepare the bread, cut a circle from the top of the loaf. Pull out the bread from the center of the loaf to make room for the dip. Pour the hot dip into the bread bowl, replace the "lid," and serve with the extra bread.

GUACAMOLE

Makes about 1 cup (2 to 4 servings)

- 2 avocados
- 1 tablespoon lime or lemon juice
- ½ teaspoon salt
- ¼ teaspoon hot sauce (optional)

1. Cut the avocados in half and remove the pits.

2. Scoop the green part out of the skin and put it into a mixing bowl.

3. Add the lime or lemon juice, salt, and hot sauce, if using, and mash with the back of a fork until the guacamole is smooth and creamy.

Chef's Notes

Avocados are ripe and ready to make guacamole when they are soft to the touch and have the texture of a banana.

You can add many other ingredients to guacamole, such as cilantro, minced garlic, chopped tomatoes, and sour cream or yogurt.

Using Acid to Keep an Avocado from Browning

Adding lemon or lime juice to avocado after cutting it prevents the avocado from losing its bright green color and turning dark brown.

About Avocados

Although there are many varieties of avocados, two distinct types are found in our local grocery stores. Hass avocados are small (about 6 ounces), pear shaped, and have dark bumpy skin and a rich creamy flesh. Choquette, or hall, avocados are mostly grown in Florida and are large (up to 2 pounds) with bright green skin and flesh that is mild in flavor and a bit soupy when pureed. Avocados are nutritious and contain monounsaturated fat, a healthy type of fat.

TOMATO SALSA

Makes 4 to 6 servings

4 tomatoes, chopped

1 green bell pepper, chopped

1 small red onion, minced

3 tablespoons chopped fresh cilantro

1 tablespoon lime juice, plus more as needed

1 teaspoon salt, plus more as needed

1. In a medium bowl, combine the tomatoes, green pepper, onion, cilantro, lime juice, and salt. Mix well.

2. Cover and refrigerate for several hours to allow the flavor to fully develop.

3. Taste and adjust the seasoning by adding more lime juice or salt, if necessary, before serving.

Where's the Heat?

Turns out the culprit is a chemical in chile peppers called *capsaicin*. This chemical is concentrated in the inner white fibers of the pepper and also coats its seeds, with significantly less in the walls of the pepper.

The perceived "heat" of the pepper results from both the amount and the specific type of capsaicin. High temperatures, drought conditions, and nearness to full ripening all contribute to high levels of capsaicin and a correspondingly intense burst of heat! Some chiles are also genetically built to produce more of the chemical. You can remove the ribs and seeds if you want the chiles to be less spicy, or leave them in if you like them spicier.

Some common peppers include: green, red, and yellow sweet bell peppers, Anaheim, poblanos, padron, red Fresno, jalapeño, serrano, and Thai bird chiles. If you're ever using really spicy peppers, you should wear gloves and be careful not to touch your eyes or face — the capsaicin can burn your skin.

Think Like a Chef

You can make different kinds of salsa by combining different fruits, vegetables, and herbs or seasonings. Sweet and spicy flavors taste especially good together.

Corn and Black Bean Salsa: corn + black beans + minced garlic + minced jalapeño

Pineapple Salsa: diced pineapple + minced red onion + cilantro

Avocado Mango Salsa: tomato + avocado + mango + cilantro

GREEN TOMATILLO SALSA (SALSA VERDE)

Makes 1½ cups (6 servings)

10 tomatillos, husks removed, rinsed and quartered
¼ cup chopped onion
2 cloves garlic, peeled
1 teaspoon salt
½ teaspoon hot sauce, plus more as needed
½ cup cilantro leaves

1. Place the tomatillos, onion, garlic, salt, and hot sauce in a blender. Process the ingredients until they are well combined, about 1 minute.

2. Add the cilantro and puree until the salsa is very smooth.

3. Serve immediately, or cover and refrigerate for up to 2 days.

What Is a Tomatillo?

Sometimes called a Mexican green tomato, a tomatillo looks like a small green tomato with a papery covering or husk. It is in the same family as a tomato but has a distinctive tart flavor.

VEGETABLE SUMMER ROLLS WITH PEANUT DIPPING SAUCE

Makes 10 rolls

2 ounces thin rice noodles (or cooked vermicelli pasta)

2 tablespoons rice vinegar

10 summer roll wrappers (8-inch diameter rice-paper rounds)

5 leaves green leaf lettuce, cut in half

¾ cup shredded napa cabbage

⅓ cup mint leaves

⅓ cup basil leaves

⅓ cup cilantro leaves

½ cup shredded carrot

½ cup thinly sliced bell pepper, any color

Peanut Dipping Sauce, for serving (recipe follows)

1. Cover the rice noodles with hot water and soak until tender, about 15 minutes. Drain the noodles, transfer them to a bowl, and then stir in the vinegar. (Skip the soaking step if using cooked vermicelli pasta.)

2. Fill a shallow dish with warm water.

3. Working with 1 wrapper at a time, soak the wrapper in the water until it is pliable, 30 to 45 seconds, then transfer to a plate lined with damp paper towels. Place 1 piece of lettuce on the rice paper, and top with the cabbage, mint, basil, cilantro, carrot, bell pepper, and noodles in a line.

4. Fold the edges of the rice paper in toward the center. Then, working away from yourself, tightly roll the wrapper around the filling. Set on a plate with the seam side facing down. Repeat with the remaining rice papers and fillings.

5. Cut the rolls in half and serve with the peanut dipping sauce.

PEANUT DIPPING SAUCE

Makes 1 cup

2 teaspoons peanut oil

2 teaspoons red curry paste

¼ cup peanut butter

¼ cup coconut milk

¼ cup water

3 tablespoons fresh lime juice

1 tablespoon sweet Thai chili sauce (optional)

1. Heat the oil in a medium saucepan over medium heat. Add the curry paste and cook until the paste bubbles slightly, about 1 minute.

2. Add the peanut butter, coconut milk, water, lime juice, and chili sauce, if using, and reduce the heat to low. Cook, stirring constantly, for 3 minutes. When the liquid begins to bubble, remove it from the heat and continue to stir for 1 minute. Let cool completely before serving.

Chef's Note

Red curry paste is available in Asian markets and some supermarkets.

SWEET SNACKS AND DESSERTS

Applesauce

Raspberry Shaved Ice

Piña Colada Ice Pops

Hazelnut Chocolate Spread

Instant Hot Chocolate Mix

Chocolate Chunk Cookies

Chewy Graham Crackers

Nut Butter Cookies

Pound Cake

Vanilla Pudding

Kaleigh's New York–Style Krumb Cake

Flourless Chocolate Cake

Applesauce Loaf Cake

Dutch Apple Cake

Hot Fudge Sauce

Strawberry Sauce

Vanilla or Chocolate Oreo Shake

Frozen "Hot" Chocolate

Oreo Ice Cream "Cake"

Apple Hand Pies

Pie Dough

APPLESAUCE

Makes 4 cups

10 apples, any variety

4 tablespoons water

3 tablespoons light brown sugar

2 teaspoons ground cinnamon (optional)

1. Peel the apples and cut them in half from the top to the bottom. Scoop out the cores with a spoon and cut each half into about 10 pieces.

2. Place the apples in a large saucepan and add the water, brown sugar, and cinnamon, if using.

3. Cover the pan and cook over low heat until the apples are soft and saucy, about 30 minutes. Remove from the heat and let cool.

4. If you'd like, you can mash the applesauce with a potato masher, puree it with a stick blender, or leave it chunky.

5. Transfer the cooled applesauce to a covered container and refrigerate.

Turning Applesauce into Apple Butter

Apple butter is a condensed applesauce made by cooking apples slowly with cider or water for a long time, to the point where the sugar in the apples caramelizes, turning the apple butter a deep brown color. The concentration of sugar makes apple butter keep longer than applesauce. To make it, continue to cook the applesauce on low heat, stirring occasionally, until very thick, about 30 to 40 minutes. Apple butter is delicious on toast, as a sandwich spread, mixed into yogurt, or eaten with cheese and crackers.

Think like a Chef

Don't just stop at plain applesauce — try other fruits too.

Cherry Applesauce: apples + cherries

Pear Sauce: pears + grated fresh ginger

RASPBERRY SHAVED ICE

Makes 6 cups

3 cups raspberry jam or jelly
3 cups water
1 cup sugar
1 tablespoon fresh lemon juice

1. Place a 9-by-13-inch pan or a freezer-safe bowl in the freezer to chill.

2. In a large bowl, combine the jam, water, sugar, and lemon juice. Stir until blended and the sugar has dissolved.

3. Pour into the chilled pan or bowl and place in the freezer overnight, until it is completely frozen.

4. To serve, use a fork to shave ice off of the frozen block. It is best to shave just what you need and to leave the block frozen until the next time. Cover the pan or bowl with plastic wrap in between uses.

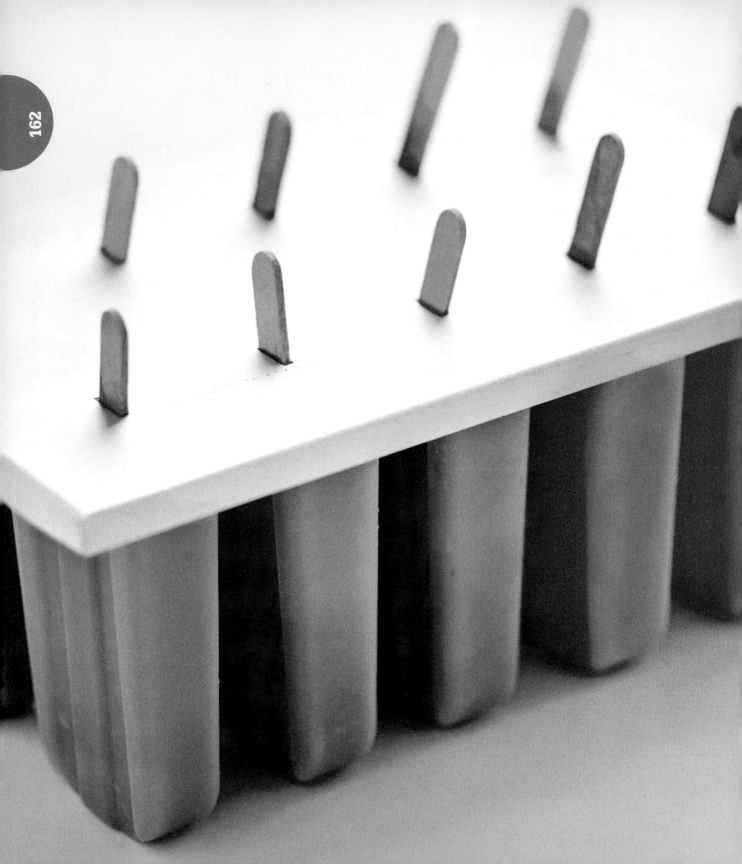

PIÑA COLADA ICE POPS

Makes 6 to 8 ice pops, depending on the mold size

1 cup pineapple chunks (fresh or canned)
¾ cup milk
½ cup orange or pineapple juice
4 tablespoons coconut milk
4 tablespoons sugar

1. Combine the pineapple, milk, juice, coconut milk, and sugar in a blender and puree until smooth, about 1 minute.

2. Pour the mixture into ice pop molds and freeze until solid, 4 to 6 hours.

How to Cut a Pineapple

Place the pineapple on its side on the cutting board and remove the stalk. Cut off the top of the pineapple, then cut off the bottom. Stand the pineapple up and cut the skin off of the sides in strips, working your way all around the pineapple until you have cut off all the skin. You should now have a cylinder of pineapple flesh. You will probably have some divots left (also called eyes—the firm brown spots on the sides). Remove these with a melon baller or potato peeler. Place the pineapple on its side and begin cutting slices. The thickness is up to you. Work your way down the pineapple until you've sliced up the entire thing. The core in the middle of the pineapple will be pretty hard. Taking a slice firmly in your hand, cut around the core. Once you've cut all the way around the core, use your fingers to dislodge it. Cut the pineapple slices into chunks.

Think Like a Chef

Any pureed fruit can be used to make ice pops.

Watermelon Ice Pops: watermelon + lime juice + mint

Peach and Blackberry Ice Pops: peaches + blackberries

Raspberry Lemonade Ice Pops: raspberries + lemonade

Cherry Ginger Ice Pops: cherries + grated fresh ginger + ginger ale

HAZELNUT CHOCOLATE SPREAD

Makes 2 cups

- 2 cups raw hazelnuts
- 1½ cups confectioners' sugar
- ½ cup unsweetened cocoa powder
- ⅛ teaspoon salt
- 4 tablespoons vegetable oil
- ½ teaspoon vanilla extract

1. Preheat the oven to 400°F.

2. Spread the hazelnuts on a baking sheet and roast until the nuts are golden brown, about 10 minutes.

3. Meanwhile, whisk together the confectioners' sugar, cocoa powder, and salt in a medium bowl and set aside.

4. Place the roasted hazelnuts in a separate medium bowl. Place a plate over the bowl and shake the bowl rapidly up and down to loosen the skins of the nuts. Remove any remaining skins by rubbing the nuts in a dry kitchen towel or between clean hands.

5. Process the nuts in a food processor, occasionally scraping down the sides of the container, until smooth. Once the nuts become smooth, add the oil and vanilla and continue to process, scraping down the container until you achieve the consistency of peanut butter. Add the cocoa mixture and process until well combined. Store the spread in an airtight container in the refrigerator.

Chef's Note

The time it takes for the hazelnuts to become a smooth puree will depend on the speed and power of your food processor. It may take more time than you expect for the nuts to become creamy.

Did You Know?

The Northwest Italian region of Piedmont is the original source of the hazelnut spread Nutella, which was invented in the 1940s by a pastry chef named Pietro Ferrero. According to the company's history, World War II rationing of chocolate and cocoa led Ferrero to experiment with extending the chocolate by pureeing it with the local hazelnuts. The result was a delicious spread that took the world by storm.

INSTANT HOT CHOCOLATE MIX

Makes twenty 1-cup servings

3 cups confectioners' sugar
1 cup unsweetened cocoa powder
1 cup powdered milk
1 tablespoon cornstarch
Pinch of salt

Into a large bowl, sift together the confectioners' sugar, cocoa powder, powdered milk, cornstarch, and salt. Whisk to combine. Store in an airtight container at room temperature.

To Make Hot Cocoa

For individual servings, carefully mix together 1 cup of boiling water or milk with ¼ cup of the cocoa mix, stirring well to incorporate.

CHOCOLATE CHUNK COOKIES

Makes about 3 dozen cookies

1 cup (2 sticks) unsalted butter

1¼ cups granulated sugar

¾ cup light brown sugar

2 eggs, beaten

2 teaspoons vanilla extract

3 cups all-purpose flour

1 teaspoon baking soda

¾ teaspoon salt

1½ cups chocolate chunks or chips

1. Preheat the oven to 375°F. Line cookie sheets with parchment paper.

2. In the bowl of an electric mixer fitted with the paddle or beater attachment, cream together the butter, granulated sugar, and brown sugar on medium speed, scraping down the bottom of the bowl at least once, until the mixture is smooth and light in color, about 3 minutes.

3. Slowly add the eggs and mix until fully incorporated, about 1 minute. Scrape the bowl and add the vanilla. Mix to combine.

4. In a medium bowl, sift together the flour, baking soda, and salt. With the mixer stopped, add the dry ingredients to the bowl, then mix on the slowest setting until the flour is just barely incorporated, about 30 seconds.

5. Add the chocolate chunks and mix on medium speed until they are evenly combined, about 30 seconds.

6. Form the dough into balls the size of golf balls and space them evenly on the prepared cookie sheets, leaving about 3 inches between each cookie.

7. Bake until golden brown around the edges, 12 to 14 minutes. Let cool completely on the cookie sheets.

Think Like a Chef

Instead of semisweet chocolate chips, you could add milk or white chocolate, dried fruit, and/or nuts to your cookies. Just use approximately the same amount as in the recipe here. Try adding candies such as M&M's or candy corn, or a combination of white chocolate chips and dried cherries.

Chef's Note

You can make your own frozen cookie dough to bake later: Shape the cookie dough into logs, roll in plastic wrap or wax paper, and freeze for up to 4 months. To bake cookies, cut ¼-inch slices, arrange on a baking sheet, and follow Step 7, baking for 3 to 4 minutes longer.

Kitchen Vocabulary

Creaming butter and sugar means to beat them until they are very light and fluffy.

Why Do I Add Salt to Sweet Food?

Adding salt to a sweet food, in moderation, brings out the other flavors within the food.

Fun Fact

In early times, the only sweetener used in baking was honey. Extracting and crystallizing sugar from sugar cane was a slow process, and sugar's high price meant that it was used sparingly. In 1492, Columbus is said to have brought the first sugar cane to the New World, which in part led to the colonization of the Caribbean, where it grew so well. Sugar quickly spread to every continent, which lowered its price and made it available to the masses.

CHEWY GRAHAM CRACKERS

Makes 8 to 12 cookies, depending on the size

2¼ cups all-purpose flour

1 teaspoon baking soda

¼ teaspoon salt

¼ cup honey

¼ cup milk

2 teaspoons vanilla extract

½ cup (1 stick) unsalted butter, room temperature

¼ cup plus 1 tablespoon granulated sugar

¾ cup light brown sugar

½ teaspoon ground cinnamon

1. In a medium bowl, sift together the flour, baking soda, and salt. In a separate bowl, combine the honey, milk, and vanilla.

2. Using an electric mixer fitted with the paddle or beater attachment, cream the butter together with ¼ cup of the granulated sugar and the light brown sugar on medium speed, scraping down the bowl with a rubber spatula, until the mixture is light and fluffy, about 3 minutes.

3. Reduce the mixer to low speed and add the flour mixture in two parts, alternating with the honey mixture, until all of the ingredients are added and the dough is smooth, about 1 minute.

4. Remove the dough from the bowl and shape it into a rectangle, wrap it in plastic wrap, and refrigerate until firm, about 45 minutes.

5. Meanwhile, preheat the oven to 350°F.

6. Lightly grease an 8-by-12-inch baking sheet and press the dough evenly onto the pan.

7. In a small bowl, combine the remaining tablespoon of granulated sugar with the cinnamon and press it onto the top of the dough. Use a knife to cut the dough into 8 or 12 even squares.

8. Poke each square with a fork several times to create holes in the tops of the cookies.

9. Bake until the cookies are golden brown, about 15 minutes. Let cool in the pan.

NUT BUTTER COOKIES

Makes 2 dozen cookies

1¼ cups all-purpose flour

½ teaspoon baking powder

½ teaspoon baking soda

¼ teaspoon salt

½ cup nut or seed butter, such as peanut, sunflower, almond, or soy

½ cup (1 stick) unsalted butter, room temperature

½ cup light brown sugar

1 egg

½ teaspoon vanilla extract

1 tablespoon granulated sugar, for sprinkling

1. Preheat the oven to 350°F.

2. In a medium bowl, whisk together the flour, baking powder, baking soda, and salt.

3. In a separate bowl, using an electric mixer fitted with the paddle or beater attachment, cream together the nut butter, butter, and brown sugar until light and creamy, about 3 minutes. Scrape down the bottom and side of the bowl with a rubber spatula as needed to make sure all of the ingredients are fully incorporated.

4. Add the egg and vanilla and mix until combined, scraping down the bowl as necessary, about 1 minute.

5. On low speed, mix in the dry ingredients just until incorporated, scraping down the bowl as needed.

6. Using a tablespoon measure, scoop the dough onto a baking sheet, leaving about 1 inch of space between each cookie. Gently press a fork into the top of each cookie to make a crisscross pattern (dipping the fork in water might help to prevent sticking), and sprinkle with the granulated sugar.

7. Bake the cookies until golden brown around the edges, 10 to 12 minutes. Transfer the finished cookies to a rack to cool.

POUND CAKE

Makes one 9-by-5-inch loaf

1¾ cups all-purpose flour

1 teaspoon baking powder

½ teaspoon salt

1 cup (2 sticks) unsalted butter,
room temperature

1 cup sugar

4 eggs, room temperature

½ teaspoon vanilla extract

1. Preheat the oven to 350°F, and lightly grease a
9-by-5-inch loaf pan.

2. In a medium bowl, whisk together the flour,
baking powder, and salt.

3. Using an electric mixer fitted with the paddle
or beater attachment, cream together the butter
and sugar on medium speed until light and fluffy,
about 3 minutes. Scrape down the bottom and
side of the bowl with a rubber spatula as needed
during mixing to ensure all of the ingredients are
fully incorporated.

4. Slowly beat in the eggs one at a time, scraping
down the bowl as necessary and allowing each
egg to fully mix into the batter before adding
the next.

5. Reduce the speed of the mixer to low and
mix in the dry ingredients and vanilla extract,
scraping down the bowl as necessary, until just
incorporated, about 2 minutes.

6. Pour the batter into the prepared loaf pan and
bake until a toothpick inserted into the center
comes out clean, about 45 minutes.

7. Allow the cake to cool slightly in the pan. Run
a knife between the cake and the sides of the
pan, invert onto a wire cooling rack, and let cool
completely before serving.

Chef's Note

Mix in the eggs slowly, or the temperature of the eggs
may cause the batter to separate.

Did You Know?

The original pound cake recipe was easy to remember
because it used a pound of each main ingredient
(butter, sugar, eggs, and flour). This recipe has been
reduced by half from the original, so now it should be
called a half-pound cake!

Think Like a Chef

To make different kinds of pound
cake, you can add in about ¼ cup
of any chunky ingredient, such as
chocolate chips, dried or chopped fresh
fruit, or shredded coconut.

Coconut Macaroon Pound Cake:
coconut + dark chocolate

Apple Streusel Pound Cake: chopped
apples + cinnamon + raisins + Crumb
Topping (page 173)

Think Like a Chef

In addition to changing the flavors in your pound cake, you can also serve it in a lot of ways, to come up with all sorts of new desserts.

Grilled Pound Cake with Strawberry Sauce: sliced, grilled Pound Cake + Strawberry Sauce (page 178) + sliced strawberries + whipped cream (see page 180)

Pound Cake Ice Cream Cake: sliced Pound Cake + softened ice cream + crushed candy bars + whipped cream (see page 180)

Pudding Trifle: cubed Pound Cake + Vanilla Pudding (page 172) + raspberries + chocolate shavings

VANILLA PUDDING

Makes 6 servings

2 cups milk

1 cup sugar

Pinch of salt

3 tablespoons cornstarch

2 egg yolks

1 tablespoon unsalted butter

1 teaspoon vanilla extract

1. Combine 1 cup of the milk, ½ cup of the sugar, and the salt in a medium saucepan and bring to a boil over medium heat, stirring gently with a wooden spoon.

2. Meanwhile, in a medium bowl, combine the cornstarch with the remaining ½ cup sugar. Stirring with a whisk, add the remaining cup of milk. Add the egg yolks, stirring with the whisk until the mixture is completely smooth.

3. Slowly add about one third of the hot milk to the bowl, stirring constantly with the whisk. This is called tempering. Return the tempered egg mixture to the remaining hot milk in the saucepan. Continue cooking, stirring constantly with the whisk, until the pudding comes to a boil. Remove from the heat and stir in the butter and vanilla.

4. Pour into serving dishes and cover, pressing plastic wrap directly on the surface of the pudding to prevent a skin from forming. Refrigerate until fully chilled.

Kitchen Vocabulary

Tempering means to add a small amount of hot liquid to the eggs before you combine the whole mixture. This allows the temperature of the eggs to rise slowly so they do not "scramble."

KALEIGH'S NEW YORK–STYLE KRUMB CAKE

Makes one 9-by-12-inch cake

Cake Batter

1½ cups all-purpose flour

½ cup sugar

2½ teaspoons baking powder

½ teaspoon salt

½ cup milk

1 egg

2 tablespoons vegetable oil

1 teaspoon vanilla extract

Crumb Topping

2½ cups all-purpose flour

1 cup packed light brown sugar

1½ teaspoons ground cinnamon

¼ teaspoon salt

1 cup (2 sticks) unsalted butter, melted

Confectioners' sugar, for dusting

1. Preheat the oven to 325°F. Lightly oil a 9-by-12-inch baking pan.

2. To make the cake batter, in a medium bowl, sift together the flour, sugar, baking powder, and salt.

3. In a second bowl, mix together the milk, egg, oil, and vanilla.

4. Stir the wet ingredients into the dry ingredients until fully blended.

5. Using a rubber spatula, spread the batter into the prepared pan.

6. To make the crumb topping, in a medium bowl, mix together the flour, sugar, cinnamon, salt, and butter.

7. Sprinkle the crumb topping over the batter in the cake pan.

8. Bake until golden brown and a toothpick inserted in the center of the cake comes out clean, about 20 minutes.

9. Let the cake cool completely on a wire rack. Dust with confectioners' sugar before serving.

FLOURLESS CHOCOLATE CAKE

Makes one 9-inch cake

1 cup sugar

½ cup water

1 pound semisweet chocolate, chopped (or chocolate chips)

1 cup (2 sticks) unsalted butter, softened

1 tablespoon vanilla extract

6 eggs

2 tablespoons confectioners' sugar, for dusting

1. Preheat the oven to 300°F. Lightly grease a 9-inch round cake pan. Cut a circle of parchment paper to fit the bottom of the pan, and press it into place.

2. In a small saucepan over high heat, bring the sugar and water to a boil, stirring to dissolve the sugar. Turn off the heat and add the chocolate, stirring with a wooden spoon until fully melted.

3. Add the butter and vanilla to the chocolate mixture and stir until the butter is melted. Let the mixture cool completely.

4. Using an electric mixer fitted with the paddle or beater attachment, beat the eggs on high speed until they are lighter in color and creamy, 3 to 4 minutes.

5. Reduce the mixer speed to low and slowly add the chocolate mixture, mixing just until the chocolate is fully incorporated, about 30 seconds. Pour the cake batter into the prepared cake pan.

6. Bake the cake until the sides of the cake look firm and set, but the center still appears slightly wet, about 1 hour.

7. Remove from the oven and let cool completely before removing from the pan. Dust with confectioners' sugar and serve.

APPLESAUCE LOAF CAKE

Makes one 8-by-5-inch loaf

1¾ cups all-purpose flour

1 teaspoon baking soda

1 teaspoon baking powder

1 teaspoon ground cinnamon

½ teaspoon salt

¼ teaspoon ground allspice

½ cup (1 stick) unsalted butter, room temperature

1 cup sugar

1 egg

1 teaspoon vanilla extract

1 cup Applesauce (page 160)

1. Preheat the oven to 350°F.

2. Grease and lightly flour an 8-by-5-inch loaf pan to keep the cake from sticking.

3. In a small bowl, whisk together the flour, baking soda, baking powder, cinnamon, salt, and allspice.

4. In the bowl of an electric mixer fitted with the paddle or beater attachment, cream together the butter and sugar on medium speed, scraping down the bottom of the bowl at least once, until the mixture is smooth and light in color, about 3 minutes.

5. Add the egg and vanilla extract and mix until the mixture is smooth, scraping down the side of the bowl as needed to ensure everything is fully incorporated, about 1 minute.

6. Add half of the flour mixture and mix just until combined, scraping down the bowl as needed. Add half of the applesauce, and mix until combined.

7. Add the remaining flour and the remaining applesauce, mixing until combined after each. Mix on low speed until the ingredients are well incorporated and the batter is smooth, about 3 minutes.

8. Pour the batter into the prepared loaf pan and bake until a toothpick inserted into the center of the cake comes out clean, about 45 minutes.

9. Remove the cake from the oven and allow to cool slightly in the pan. Run a knife between the cake and the sides of the pan to loosen, then flip it over to remove the cake and place onto a cooling rack. Let cool completely before serving.

DUTCH APPLE CAKE

Makes one 9-inch cake

½ cup (1 stick) unsalted butter, room temperature

1 cup plus 3 tablespoons granulated sugar

2 eggs, beaten

2 cups all-purpose flour

1 tablespoon baking powder

1 teaspoon salt

1 cup milk

1 teaspoon vanilla extract

2 Granny Smith apples

1 teaspoon ground cinnamon

2 tablespoons confectioners' sugar, for dusting

1. Preheat the oven to 350°F.

2. Lightly butter or oil the bottom and side of an 9-inch round cake pan and dust with flour.

3. In the bowl of an electric mixer fitted with the paddle or beater attachment, cream together the butter and 1 cup of the granulated sugar on medium speed, scraping down the bottom of the bowl at least once, until the mixture is smooth and light in color, about 3 minutes.

4. Slowly add the eggs and mix until fully incorporated, about 1 minute. Scrape the bowl as needed during mixing to ensure everything is fully incorporated.

5. In a small bow, mix together the flour, baking powder, and salt.

6. Add the dry ingredients, alternating with the milk, to the butter and sugar, mixing until just incorporated, about 2 minutes. Scrape down the side and bottom of the bowl with a rubber spatula. Add the vanilla and mix for 1 more minute on low speed. Pour the batter into the prepared cake pan.

7. Peel the apples and cut each one into 8 wedges, removing the core. Press the apple pieces into the top of the batter so just their tops are showing.

8. Mix together the remaining 3 tablespoons of granulated sugar and the cinnamon and sprinkle evenly over the top of the cake.

9. Bake for about 45 minutes, or until a toothpick inserted into the center comes out clean.

10. Cool in the pan for 15 minutes on a cake rack and then remove from the pan to cool completely.

11. Dust with confectioners' sugar and serve.

Chef's Note
To dust the top of the cake with confectioners' sugar, put the sugar in a fine-mesh sieve. Hold the sieve over the cake, and gently tap the edge of the sieve to shake out the sugar.

HOT FUDGE SAUCE

Makes about ¾ cup

¼ cup milk

1 cup semisweet chocolate chips

¼ cup light corn syrup

¼ teaspoon vanilla extract

1. In a small saucepan over medium heat, heat the milk until it just begins to simmer.

2. Remove the pan from the heat, add the chocolate chips and corn syrup, and stir continuously until the chocolate is melted, about 3 minutes. Add the vanilla and stir to incorporate.

3. Serve immediately, or transfer to a covered container and refrigerate until ready to use.

4. To reheat the sauce, spoon the hot fudge into a microwave-safe container and heat in 10-second intervals until warm. (The total amount of time needed will depend on the amount of sauce.)

STRAWBERRY SAUCE

Makes 6 to 8 servings

2 cups strawberries, fresh or frozen

¼ cup sugar

2 to 3 tablespoons water, plus more as needed

1. Use a small knife to cut the stems from the strawberries (if fresh).

2. In a small bowl, mix the strawberries with the sugar and let sit for about 1 hour, until the strawberries have softened and there is red juice in the bottom of the bowl.

3. Transfer the strawberries to a blender and add the water. Puree until the mixture is smooth. If the sauce is too thick, add more water 1 tablespoon at a time until it is saucy.

4. Serve immediately, or refrigerate the sauce in a covered container until ready to use.

Chef's Note

If you are using fresh strawberries, you'll need less water than if using frozen berries, so start with 1 tablespoon and add more, 1 tablespoon at a time, until the sauce reaches the consistency you'd like.

VANILLA OR CHOCOLATE OREO SHAKE

Makes 5 cups

3 cups ice

2 cups milk

8 Oreo cookies

6 tablespoons sugar

2 tablespoons unsweetened cocoa powder (optional)

2 teaspoons vanilla extract

1. In a blender, combine the ice, milk, cookies, sugar, cocoa powder, if using, and vanilla and puree until smooth.

2. Serve right away in chilled tall glasses.

FROZEN "HOT" CHOCOLATE

Makes 4 servings

8 large marshmallows

2 cups ice

1½ cups milk

4 tablespoons sugar

2 tablespoons unsweetened cocoa powder

¼ teaspoon vanilla extract

1. Thread the marshmallows onto a metal or bamboo skewer. Turn a stove burner on low and toast the marshmallows over the flame until they are brown and beginning to puff. Set the toasted marshmallows aside.

2. In a blender, combine the ice, milk, sugar, cocoa powder, and vanilla. Puree until smooth, about 1 minute.

3. When the drink is smooth, add 4 of the toasted marshmallows and puree for a few seconds, just to combine.

4. Pour into mugs and garnish with the remaining toasted marshmallows.

Safety First

This recipe calls for cooking the marshmallows over a flame, which could be dangerous. Get permission to use the stove before you start.

OREO ICE CREAM "CAKE"

Makes 12 servings

2 quarts vanilla ice cream

20 Oreo cookies

1 can whipped cream (or 4 cups homemade Chantilly Cream, recipe follows)

Sprinkles, candy, or chocolate sauce, for decoration

1. Remove the ice cream from the freezer and let it soften so it is easier to scoop.

2. Place the Oreos in a zip-top bag or a bowl and crush them using a rolling pin or your fist.

3. Line the pan of your choice (see Chef's Note) with plastic wrap. Working quickly, scoop half of the ice cream into the lined pan and then sprinkle half of the crushed cookies randomly over the cake.

4. Add the remaining ice cream to the pan and smooth and level the surface using a rubber spatula.

5. Press the remaining crushed cookies evenly onto the top of the cake (this will end up being the bottom of the cake when the cake is inverted for serving). Cover the pan with wax paper and plastic wrap and freeze until firm, at least 6 hours or overnight.

6. To remove the cake from the pan, place it in a shallow container of hot water to melt the edges.

7. Remove the plastic wrap and wax paper, flip the cake over onto a serving platter, and remove the pan. Pull off the plastic wrap.

8. Frost the cake with the whipped cream and decorate it with sprinkles, candy, or chocolate sauce. Serve immediately.

Chef's Note

This recipe will make just over 8 cups of ice cream "batter," and it can be made in a variety of cake pans, bowls, or serving dishes. Choose one that will hold 10 to 12 cups, and make sure it fits into the freezer.

CHANTILLY CREAM (SWEETENED WHIPPED CREAM)

Makes 2 cups

1 cup cold heavy cream

2 tablespoons confectioners' sugar

¾ teaspoon vanilla extract

In a medium bowl, whisk the cream by hand until it forms medium peaks. Add the confectioners' sugar and vanilla and continue to whisk until the cream forms stiff peaks. Use immediately, or refrigerate until ready to use.

APPLE HAND PIES

Makes 16 pies

2 tablespoons unsalted butter

3 Granny Smith apples, peeled, cored, and chopped

½ cup sugar

½ teaspoon salt

¼ teaspoon ground cinnamon

1½ teaspoons vanilla extract

Pie Dough (page 183)

2 eggs, beaten, for brushing

Coarse sanding sugar, as needed

1. Preheat the oven to 375°F. Line two baking sheets with parchment paper.

2. In a large sauté pan, melt the butter over medium-high heat. Add the apples and cook, stirring with a wooden spoon, until they begin to soften, 5 to 6 minutes. Add the sugar, salt, and cinnamon. Cook, stirring, until the sugar dissolves and begins to caramelize and the apples are cooked through, 4 to 5 minutes more. Remove from the heat and stir in the vanilla. Transfer the apple mixture to a bowl to cool.

3. On a lightly floured surface, divide the dough into two pieces. Roll each piece of dough, one at a time, until it is about ⅛ inch thick. Using a 3½-inch cookie cutter (or a glass of about the same size), cut 32 circles from the dough.

4. Brush the outside edge of half of the dough circles with the beaten eggs. Spoon about 1½ tablespoons of apple filling into the middle of each of the circles with the brushed edges. Set the remaining dough circles on top. Use a fork to press around the edge of each pie to push out any excess air and seal the seams.

5. Place the hand pies on the prepared baking sheets. Brush the tops of the pies with the remaining beaten eggs and sprinkle with sanding sugar. With a small knife, carefully cut a 1-inch slit in the top of each pie.

6. Bake until the pies are golden brown, about 15 minutes. Let cool on the baking sheets and serve warm or at room temperature.

Chef's Note

You could also fold the dough circles in half to make semicircle-shaped hand pies, and sprinkle the tops with granulated sugar or even cinnamon-sugar instead of coarse sanding sugar.

PIE DOUGH

Makes enough for 16 hand pies, two 9-inch single-crust pies, or 1 double-crust pie

2½ cups all-purpose flour

2 teaspoons salt

1 cup (2 sticks) unsalted butter, cold, cut into ½-inch cubes

½ cup cold water

1. Combine the flour and salt in the bowl of a food processor and pulse for 3 seconds to combine.

2. Add half of the cold butter. Pulse for 3 to 5 seconds, or until the butter is the size of peas.

3. Add the remaining butter and pulse for 3 seconds.

4. Add the water, a few tablespoons at a time, until the dough begins to form a ball.

5. Wrap the dough in plastic wrap and chill it in the refrigerator for at least 1 hour before using, or freeze it to use later (let it thaw in the refrigerator overnight before using).

INDEX

Note: Page references in *italics* indicate photographs.